Reading Shtisel

A Television Masterpiece from Israel

by

Maurice Yacowar

Second, expanded edition

published lulu.com

Introduction

Since its debut on Israeli television in June, 2013, the drama series *Shtisel* has enjoyed remarkable success. It won immediate attention and grew in ambition and consequence through a second season in 2015. Netflix brought it to North America in 2018.

The drama now stands as a two-season epic, developed over two 12-episode arcs. Each 45-minute episode, carefully constructed, interweaves two or three plot-lines. The drama follows the concerns of a Haredi (ultra-orthodox) Jewish family in the Geula neighbourhood in Jerusalem. That location borders upon the even more extreme Mea She'arim. We're not at the end of that spectrum.

The opening title sequence — repeated each episode — establishes the drama's two settings. The physical is the neighbourhood street scenes — daily life represented by laundry blowing above the street, the jam of stone walls, poster bulletins, murky windows. Various orthodox men stroll through, including the man we will meet as Shulem Shtisel (Doval'e Glickman), smoking, looking sage.

The psychological setting centers on his son Akiva (Michael Aloni). Foreshadowing his artistic ambition, he views the world through his rolled-up sketchbook, but drops it when bumped by a passerby. Shulem puts his hand on Akiva's back as they start up a staircase. The hand could be support or a slap.

Avi Belleli's song over the titles establishes the theme of disintegration: "Where is everyone suddenly going? Everything is pulling away and disappearing....Where do we continue from here, to where?"[1]

This ephemerality contrasts to the characters' most frequent blessing. Every ingestion of food or drink is preceded with "Blessed are you, God, at whose word all came to be." Against the passing of human life, the prayer reaffirms the everlasting Creator. At every entry and exit the characters kiss the *mezuzah* (a small case containing the *Shema* prayer) on the door jamb. These blessings connect the ephemeral human to the eternal divine.

---

[1] This translation comes from Mark L. Levinson on the *Quora* website.

In addition to the odd scene of home services — *e.g.*, the men's morning prayers, the lighting of the Sabbath candles, the home funeral services (*shiva*) — we get only one synagogue service: Zelig's circumcision, where the naming is crucial to the plot (season II, episode 2; *i.e.*, II,2). Why no more synagogue scenes? The story is about the characters' daily lives, not their periodic festivals, not their religion. This drama is scrupulously constructed to omit anything that doesn't advance its themes. Correspondingly, we can expect every detail to be functional, to connect to something else in the structure. Unlike life, nothing here just "happens," *sans* significance.

Hence the austerity in the musical score. What rare song arises within the narrative has been selected for its pertinent lyrics. The external music tends to be spare, bare notes on the piano or guitar, far from the traditional film scores that amplify the emotions. The usual Jewish narrative music — think the *yiddle* with a fiddle, the mournful fellow with the cello — is rare here.

Shulem is the *pater familias* — and the show's primary target of analysis and satire. He's a 62-year old Talmud Torah teacher, recently widowed. Though a gentle teacher, a major theme is the harm he has done his children. "Shulem" is not quite Sholom, *i.e.*, not quite "peace" (a distinction drawn in I,10). He is similarly "off" as a father, a husband, a *mentsch* (humane being). "Shalom" also signifies wholeness, another quality which this character increasingly reveals himself lacking (especially in II,12).[2]

Our central figure of sympathy/identification is his youngest son Akiva. At 27 he still lives with his father, who disdains Akiva's ardor for art and nudges him both into a teaching career and into a conventional arranged marriage. Akiva's name connotes protection and shelter, which his ensuing romantic relationships will find him either receiving or providing. Suggesting a possible religious destiny, Rabbi Akiva was one of the greatest sages of early rabbinic study.

When Shulem's daughter Giti (Neta Riskin) is abandoned by her husband, she struggles to raise their five children on insufficient means. Her resourcefulness is limned in her name, denoting "grape

---

[2] For suggestions on the characters' names I thank my friend Lynn Greenhough.

presser." She is helped by her 13-year-old daughter Ruchami (Shira Haas, who was 18 in the first season).

The series reveals the parallel life that the Haredim live in contemporary Israel. The men and women sit separated in religious services. The men wear stark black suits and hats, their women snoods and wigs. Their interaction is rigidly proscribed.

The orthodox community's special privileges date back to Israel's founding president David Ben-Gurion in 1948. He expected Israel to become a secular state and that Orthodox Judaism would eventually disappear. To ease this evolution he granted the orthodox community several special rights, which they still enjoy even as their numbers increase dramatically. They are exempt from the military draft. The men can devote themselves to state-supported rabbinical study. Studying religion can be a full-time, sparsely paid, job. They're called "Reb" or "Rabbi" as *Talmud* scholars, not for leading a congregation.

The language catches another division in Israel. The grandparents speak the Yiddish of their European origin,. The children speak Hebrew, the historic Biblical language the Jews resurrected for their new state. The parents speak both — especially Yiddish when they don't want their children to understand.[3]

No Haredim were involved in this drama's creation, though scriptwriters Ori Elon and Yehonatan Indursky know the culture. Israel's orthodox communities may have worried about the TV series. An early shoot was reportedly interrupted by a protest when a woman applied make-up to a male actor's face. But the community was in general won over early, when it became clear that they were being treated with respect, free of the usual stereotypy.

Despite their rejection of modern media, many Haredim watched the show regularly, on TV or the internet. Indeed, a wordless tune ostensibly composed by Shulem's great-great-grandfather — but actually written for II, 9 — was played by a yeshiva band at an Orthodox (!) wedding two nights after its first telecast. Instant tradition?

---

[3] On the show's unusual use of Yiddish see Shayna Weiss, "Shtisel's Ghosts: The Politics of Yiddish in Israeli Popular Culture" (*In Geveb*, March 6, 2016).

To outsiders the drama proves a rare depiction of Israeli life apart from politics. The Independence Day episode (I,11) is perhaps the only one with a political theme, opposition to Zionism.

The show won 11 Israel Television Academy Awards. The first season's included best actor (Glickman's Shulem), director Alon Zingman and script in a Drama Series. The second included best actor (Glickman again), actress (Neta Riskin's Giti) and original music. For a climactic seal of approval: *Friends* co-creator Marta Kaufman has purchased the rights to develop an American version. With daughter Hannah K.S. Canter, Kaufman has drafted a script for the new version, set in Brooklyn. The title *Emmis* is Yiddish for "truth," not the devoutly desired TV awards.

The show also inspired two lively Facebook sites, *Shtisel: Let's Talk About It* and *Shtisel Addicts*. Unfortunately, both spurned analysis of the drama, preferring to wax appreciative and to speculate about the characters' lives outside the narrative frame, as if they were real people. Viewers who chuckled at Bubba Malka's thinking fictional TV characters were real succumbed to that naivety themselves.[4]

The show courts that error by making the characters so realistic, ensuring our emotional engagement. Even minor characters seem rounded and distinctive, like Iris, the dress-store manager for whom Giti briefly works, and Sucher, the lottery-ticket seller, fallen from the community's grace. All performances are brilliant, with nuanced expressions and gestures throughout — even in the children. Many scenes end with a close-up, the character silently showing lively interior life. The dialogue edges into poetry.

This is the magic of fiction. Dramatists invent characters to act out the play's abstract themes. They give ideas the illusion of flesh and blood. Characters should seem real but they aren't. They have no existence outside the frame of this narrative. They're fictional creations that live only here. They have no characterization or experience other than what we get here. What the writers don't tell us about them we don't need to know, to work out their meaning. Like all the other elements — setting, props, events, dialogue, music, lighting, shooting and

---

[4] An Appendix below details my banishment from these two discussion groups, with its troubling implications.

editing strategies, etc. — the characters exist only to convey the writers' themes. As a result, nothing in a play is just itself. Everything accrues a larger meaning from its context.

This is where the "reading" of my title comes in. Instead of passively receiving the play we dig into it. We work out how the separate parts relate to each other. Rather than "escape" reality we'll try to illuminate ours by thinking through what all these fictional "props" mean, how they serve the themes. This analytic approach is harder than the gut (flip emotional) response — but more rewarding.

In those themes I find a delicate balance in this drama. On the one hand, it uses a religious sect as an example of dangerous repression in a patriarchal institution, especially if it values obeying any law over compassion. The drama doesn't attack that community but analyzes the patriarchal constructions it exemplifies

The show also pays significant attention to the strengths of that firm community, the benefits it bestows on its members. This aspect poses a challenge to our alternative social construction in the West: the absolute value of unbridled individualism.

As the drama plays this theme and its manifold variations we are constantly challenged to make moral judgments. The characters' actions carry moral implications. How we respond to them tests our moral awareness. To adapt W.H. Auden's adage about a good book: We don't read the good play; it reads us. Of course, using a story to make moral points is central to Judaism — as exemplified by that great teller of instructive parables, Jesus.

The shooting budget allowed each episode the heft and polish of a feature film. Indeed, rare on TV, this series invites the shot-by-shot analysis that normally only a handful of the best feature films do. That's what attracted me to this series. Its complexity makes this the finest television drama since *The Sopranos* (the only other TV series that drew me to such an episode-by-episode study).

Like *The Sopranos*, each episode is a carefully structured advance of the overall narrative. It stands alone, usually with its own focus, while it supports the whole. The main characters are complex, conflicted, irreducible to any single trait or value. As in life, ambivalence rules. Their personal issues point to the difficult issues in contemporary life. In both series, we're plunged into a distinctive sub-culture — but one which reflects upon our own concerns. However different, they are us.

What raises the characterization beyond the usual television — and most films — is its subtlety. Rarely is a character's motivation simply stated — or simple. Often the characters behave unpredictably. We have to join the pieces to understand their choices, then proceed to their thematic implications.

Finally, in both dramas the dialogue is irresistibly funny. And often profane, given their respective characters' spirit. The brashest jokes are in Yiddish (True: I miss those in Hebrew). Thus in I,1 Rabbi Erblich's widow Shoshanna refuses to attend the famous radio rabbi's lecture in the seniors' residence lobby: "He can kiss my ass. He doesn't listen to me; why should I listen to him?" *Rebbetzin* Erblich pops up through both seasons, a frank foil to the less worldly Shtisel grandmother Malka. Erblich's quirkiness typifies the show's ability to catch life on the fly, rich even at the margins.

Then there's Akiva's yeshiva classmate Amram, who stumbles through various small background jobs under the name Farshlufen ("Sleepyhead"). This nickname suggests overall that there are characters and issues here that require some awakening. The drama's central preoccupation is how to sustain an ethical identity in a conflicted culture, whether as an individual, a family, a sect, a religion, a nation.

Season One

Episode I, 1

The opening episode establishes the series' major themes and devices, the Shtisel family members and their imminent arcs. The family/series name comes from a popular Mea She'arim restaurant. It evokes community, nourishment, perhaps the suggestion of a menu. Here is a range of family relationships and a range of restraints on the self — take your pick. Spoiler alert: This restaurant will, like the characters, reappear but transformed. The end is latent in the beginning.

In the first shot a ladle of food is dumped in a dish at Anshin's cafe.[5] This scene is revealed to be a dream when Anshin denies Akiva a pickle, it starts to snow *inside* the cafe and Akiva finds his dead mother Dvora eating near an eskimo. Dvora complains about the lack of pickles and the cold (common irritations in the afterlife). Our later visions of Dvora will bear out her name's suggestion of a bee-like industriousness, with the dedication and courage of namesake Deborah..

Starting the series with a dream is significant. The opening shot/scene usually establishes the physical world in which the story unwinds. But after this first shot, we'll have to question our bearings in every scene. This drama will shift between four levels of reality. Everything will be equally real, *i.e.*, equally unreal. The characters' daily lives will interweave with three alternative realities: their dreams, their memories (flashbacks) and their reunions with the dead. These four levels of reality within the drama point to two others outside: (i) However realistic the characters and setting, the story itself is a fiction, unreal but metaphoric. Everything embodies a larger truth. (ii) In the mystical tradition, even our "real life" this side of that fiction is itself an illusion. Our real reality awaits us in our afterlife with God. Hence the constant blessings and the kissing of the mezuzahs, which integrate the characters' material life with the spiritual. For them divinity pervades and magnifies the mundane.

The initial dreamer Akiva will prove the drama's hero, bounded by his father's domination. Though Shulem dismisses Akiva's dream as meaningless, he is troubled by it and reports it as his own — the first in his constant stream of lies — when he visits secretary Aliza Gvili for (a free) dinner. She can't explain his dream about his dead wife: "It's between you and her. Why are you asking me?" Aliza has a romantic interest in Shulem, to which he remains insensitive.

In an early indication of how loving a father Shulem will prove, he consistently diminishes Akiva — even shrinking his name to Kiva, perpetuating the childhood diminutive. In front of the students on the school trip to the zoo he scolds him: "If you want to draw the

5 Elana Horwitz advises that "Anshin" is an Aramaic Talmudic term for "people." The restaurant name connotes "Guys."

animals come on your own time." Later: "What can I say? I've totally given up on you."

Shulem treats his daughter Giti even worse. Her husband Lippe is again leaving her with their five children for six months, for his job in the Argentina branch of a Jerusalem slaughterhouse. To this unappealing prospect he has just been offered an alternative: a local electronics partnership. But when Giti seeks Shulem's help she gets his silent dismissal. Then: "Why all the fantasies all of a sudden?" "Fine. I tried." Shulem considers any off-spring's ambition a "fantasy." He expects them to live only by his.

Ominously, when Giti returns home Lippe is furtively browsing through sporty car ads. (As we later learn, Shulem made giving up his share in a car one of the conditions Lippe had to meet to marry Giti.) To keep the peace, she tells Lippe "He loves you." Lippe chafes at his father-in-law's insensitivity: "Don't worry. I'll be so rich one day he'll be asking me for money." He carries that spite to Argentina.

Shulem compounds this harshness with hypocrisy. When Aliza describes how the eskimos send their elderly off on an ice floe— in furs and with an embrace — to die in dignified reunion with nature, he recoils: "Those gentiles. Not an ounce of compassion."

This moment is rich in irony. It was set up by the surreal inclusion of an eskimo in the opening dream. In a rare cross-cultural moment, that eskimo leaves his usual fare, raw fish, and eats Anshin's deli. Of course, the eskimos are no more representative of all the gentiles than these Haredim are of all Jews. The remark confirms Shulem's insularity.

Moreover, as a culture the eskimos— more properly identified as the Inuit — are remarkably respectful of their aged. They treat them with unequalled deference in life and have a compassionate ritual for their death. They send them off with dignity and care. Given Shulem's disdain for his mother's enjoyment of her TV and his callous treatment of his children, *i.e.*, his own defining lack of compassion, he compounds his hypocrisy with self-unawareness.

This ironic moment — among many others — could be considered the heart of this episode and a driving theme for the entire series: How can any religion excuse inhumanity?

Unlike Shulem, Akiva is warm and sensitive, albeit crude with his unaccustomed authority in the classroom. When the students finally laugh at his obscure joke, he sternly silences them. He sends Israel Rotstein to the principal for drawing flip-book cartoons on his *Gemarah*. Akiva lacks his father's classroom polish, but at school lapses into his domestic authoritarianism. Shulem is kind in the class, rough at home; Akiva, the reverse. Authority is not in his nature.

Akiva has two contrasting meetings with women here. He begins the arranged date with playful concern about "the rules" that govern these meetings. Cheekily he jokes that his ambition is to become "an assistant attendant" at a *mikvah* (the Jewish ritual bath for women). Batya disqualifies herself when she agrees that his drawings — ostensibly by "a friend" — are "no big deal." Akiva deters her by claiming they will have to live with his spry father until he dies.

In contrast, when widow Elisheva Rotstein, Israel's mother, sees his sketchbook she tells her son "Your rabbi draws very well." She clearly engages with the art. The boy has already judged Akiva's art "Very professional." When Akiva suggests meeting the widow, Shulem rejects it out of hand. His NIMBY stand — Not in My *Meshpukhe* — flies in the face of the Jewish commitment to the orphan and the widow. Denied, Akiva goes to the bank where she works and invites her to a meeting. She does not appear.

Akiva's opening dream has two effects on him. At lunch he orders Anshin not to forget his pickle, as if his denial had been in life not dream. More constructively, he resolves to honour his mother's memory by establishing a free lending service— a *gemach* — for space heaters. When a soaked Elisheva comes to borrow one, she and Akiva exchange increasingly warm looks as they wait for the heater to warm up. As Akiva responds to his dream, the spiritual world can bring fear to the waking reality or it can prompt humanitarianism. Like religion.

The last scene recalls the opening dream of frigidity. The Shtisels have gathered for a dinner to mark the end of their mourning period for Dvora. They will listen to music for the first time in a year — a cassette of a boys' choir, *Pirchei Yerushalaim* singing *The Bird's Nest*. Presumably the song celebrates the warmth and security that should obtain in the Shtisel nest. From that family warmth we cut to Shulem's mother Malka in her seniors' residence room, alone.

Shulem objected to his mother getting a TV, which the Haredim reject as a secular danger. Indeed she does change, from initial shock to fascination with the outside world. At first she's disturbed that "Everything goes these days." But the human dramas catch her interest. She becomes invested in the life of an American TV family with — also forbidden in this sect — a pet dog. On *The Bold and the Beautiful* she learns their children's strange names and worries about them.

Shulem's oldest son Zvi Arye, sharing his father's rigour, disconnects Malka's set, sabotaging her pleasure. The comedic music plays this cruelty as a prank. She is left with a screen — of snow. Like Dvora in the first scene, the grandmother in the last is left with the snow, cut off from family warmth. Not just those gentiles lack compassion. The "righteous" Shulem's effect is cold *dis*-connection. He does not honour the family's Malka ("queen").

Episode I, 2

The second episode advances those warm/cold relationships. First a rabbi, then Elisheva, tell of a Japanese woman/couple accidentally electrocuted by an electric blanket. Warmth can be dangerous. This motif drives the three schisms in the episode.

The most dramatic schism is the factory manager's report that Lippe has abandoned his Judaism (including his prayer shawl, *tallis*, and skullcap, *kippah*) and his job and run off with a *shiksa* (gentile woman) in Argentina. When the manager's wife offers to establish a charity fund for Giti, she breaks down in her arms. But she won't let her call Lippe "a scoundrel," nor consider divorce. When a street crier promotes a similar charity fund Giti steels herself. She doesn't want her lot proclaimed in the streets. She tells the manager that Lippe has reported taking a better job with a Jewish diamond merchant. She doesn't need charity and asks him not to repeat his earlier "lies," *i.e.*, the truth about Lippe's abdication. As Giti maintains the illusion of their marriage, she finds no relief. Malka's American TV family may seem happy — but that husband too is unfaithful.

In the second schism, Shulem is conflicted on two fronts. First, Aliza is disturbed when Shulem criticizes her for speaking personally at school. She invited him to a concert by The Three Tenors. "Why do we have to hide?" she asks. "Coward," she concludes. On his next visit she sends him home in the rain with her leftover chicken soup instead of — as usual — inviting him in.

His second schism is with Akiva. Shulem again rejects Akiva's interest in widow Elisheva. He pretends restraint: "It's too late to educate you." Then he tries, pretending to address Akiva's classroom manner. He suggests Akiva bring banana bars to dole out pieces to students who earn a reward. That generosity would then allow him — in Shulem's sense of authority — to slap the misbehavers. That's his "important lesson in life."

To demonstrate, Shulem says the pre-punishment blessing — "I will fulfill the commitment of education" —then slaps Akiva's face. "Commitment of education" hardly justifies corporal punishment. Nor capital. He excuses his slapping his adult son as a lesson: "Know when to use the brain and when the heart." To Shulem the "brain" is following rules; the "heart," emotional instincts authority prefers to suppress.

Akiva uses this classroom lesson — more kindly. When Israel leads a class prank, Akiva calls him up, has him remove his glasses, says the punishment blessing, but instead of the slap gives him a (whole) banana bar. Whether considering the boy's mother or deciding not to be like Shulem, Akiva learned a better lesson than his father taught. His heart overrules his head, sensibly.

The third schism separates Akiva and Elisheva. Akiva uses the heater as an excuse to phone her at work. She agrees to have matchmaker Konigsberg arrange a date. Anticipating Shulem's opposition, the bookseller Konigsberg dials down the romantic: "She's like a schnitzel that was frozen, thawed, heated up, frozen, thawed, heated up in the microwave and served on a paper plate."[6] Both men who ate that schnitzel died. Compounding their separation, Elisheva lives in distant B'Nai Brak. Her home scenes alternate between her parents' Jerusalem flat and hers. She is divided in residence as in her mind to remarry — so doubly remote.

Their date discovers a natural comfort. Because he had to wait for her, she suggests he go out and return so she can wait for him.

---

6 Both Konigsberg and, later, his widow Menukha are given to comic wording and behaviour. Their tone may explain why they are named Konigsberg, Woody Allen's family name. A homage, with benefits.

Their play turns serious: She has stopped waiting for herself and now only waits for son Israel to grow up and marry. After that comfort Akiva is surprised when Konigsberg reports he has been rejected. He has other prospects for him, though, including other widows. But "twice over" is hard to find. Konigsberg treats Akiva's acceptance of one twice-wed as a requirement.

Breaching decorum, Akiva goes to Elisheva's parents to ask "what fault you have found in me. I want to marry Elisheva." As it's the Sabbath Elisheva is there. "Come inside; it's cold out there," her father greets him, then offers him tea and an unclear explanation: "Life is not that simple. People go through all sorts of things. You have to respect that." After Akiva leaves, Elisheva's mother reveals the parents didn't reject him: "I don't understand you, Elisheva."

In bed the reluctant bride listens to pop music on her radio. That's desecrating the Sabbath, she's reminded, when she meets both dead husbands at her kitchen table: "You could do with some reverence." Her first husband is religious, fondly recalling the rigours of his yeshiva days. Her second, worldlier, talks cars. The next morning she asks Israel what he thinks of his teacher Akiva. He likes him. "Like a father?" "No. Like a friend." "Yes," she agrees, "He is a child." Their age difference feeds her reluctance to undertake a third marriage. Her maturity may appeal to Akiva, having just lost his mother.

The episode closes on Akiva silently starting an arranged date with Esti Gottlieb. She's similar to Batya, pretty, but not a patch on his simpatico widow.

Perhaps Elisheva's father explained her after all. Her feelings for the younger Akiva are not enough. She lives with the memories of her past two marriages and with her son's needs. Also, the radio may suggest her wariness of Akiva's orthodoxy. She has a loophole: She didn't turn the radio on during the Sabbath, but had left it on. Some secular freedoms may tempt her more than young Akiva.

Episode I, 3

The underlying subject here is emotional vulnerability, the compulsions of the heart and its denials by "the brain," as Shulem put it (I,2). Literally: Rabbi Cheshin recovers from his heart attack so he takes his class back from Akiva. He promises not to get "upset" (*i.e.*, too emotional) again.

In Akiva's forest frolic with friends, Levi Itzhak quotes Kierkegaard's paean to the woman Regina whom he loved, got engaged to but never married: "He didn't want to be the happiest man in the world." But bachelors can fall without love, as Pinchkin scars his leg: "How the mighty art fallen." In this parable men call out for a father's/God's/comrade's help in a life of insecure footing. Akiva laughs at Pinchkin's injury, now "not the only doomed in the world."

Another friend's pragmatism unwittingly evokes Lippe's flight: "If a man drives the same Subaru for 10 years, it's only a matter of time before the radiator breaks down." Confirming this mechanistic view of marriage, Shulem admits that during his 38-year marriage he never once told Dvora he loved her. "We were together; that's all." Nor does he remember the many times she expressed her love. "What matters is only what matters." To Shulem, what matters is that she rose early every morning to warm the butter so it would spread when he returned from prayers. She served him.

Shulem remembers rejecting the ailing Dvora's request they get adjoining grave sites. She thought that "promise of longevity" might extend her life, to see Akiva married. Shulem dismissed the notion as the con of burial society thieves. To her higher faith — "Maybe there's something to it and you just don't understand." — he at last conceded.

When that and their prayers failed, Shulem retreated to religious humility: "What do we know? We know nothing." In frustration he pounds the chocolate bar machine that failed him — and Dvora's last request — like his faith.

Still denying his emotions, Shulem exploits Aliza. He drops in to sup on her left-overs. This relationship repeats his selfishness in his marriage. Hoping to justify himself, he asks if her divorced husband ever told her he loved her. He did, frequently. One of the drama's most appealing characters, the "joy" of Aliza's name confirms her function as Shulem's last opportunity for a loving marriage.

Rather than leave Akiva's love life in God's (or Akiva's) hands, Shulem promotes marriage to the Gottlieb ("God love") girl. He imposes an unwanted second date. When Akiva rejects marriage Esti manipulates him into a proposal by crying. Shulem welcomes the news uncertainly: "You did the right thing. Don't you agree?" Akiva is silent.

With Aliza, Shulem takes credit for forcing his son into a decision. She wishes Shulem would force himself into one. She is clearly frustrated by her unreciprocated commitment. "Is he happy?" she asks. Shulem: "Since when is that important? Are we supposed to be happy?" For his son's marriage Shulem imposes his will over his son's feelings: "He did what he had to do and, God willing, he'll be happy." He assumes God supports Shulem's coercion of Akiva.

At the inlaws' meeting Shulem describes Dvora as a dedicated mother and — like her favourite, Akiva — sensitive and talented. Shulem lauds her for the qualities he disdains in Akiva. The men sing of the vegetative beauty of marriage — "The mingling of the grapes, of the vine" — but the metaphor omits passion. Giti the "wine-presser" proves who does the work in these marriages. The men retreat to "It's all in God's hands." But as we'll see, it's really in the humans'.

Elisheva phones Akiva under the ruse of needing son Israel's class schedule. Having heard of Akiva's engagement she wants to hear his voice one last time. Akiva had just phoned Esti to say goodnight, himself needing reminder of her "voice like an angel" (Konigsberg). Elisheva clearly regrets losing Akiva. In God's hands their love might have thrived, but not with these interferers. Akiva runs out to find her — one last chance? — but she is gone.

Cut to Shulem scraping away at his cold butter. The episode closes on Shulem at Dvora's wardrobe, fondling her dresses, weeping. Now he expresses the emotion he denied her in life. Yet he has just manipulated his son out of a loving into an unfit engagement. Dvora would not approve this abuse of her kindred favourite.

At the inlaws' meeting there is a curious detail. Shulem claims to have six children (and 32 grandchildren). So far we have only met three — Giti, Zvi Arye and Akiva. We will later meet a daughter Racheli who escaped by marrying — a dread Chabad! So there are two children even further beyond the pale, of whom we never hear.

Sharp-eyed viewers have spotted a possible son, the bearded young man next to Akiva at the dinner ending the mourning period (I, 1). A daughter could be the younger woman at the family meeting over Shulem's possible room-mate (I,5). Their remoteness from us suggests a remoteness from Shulem. The story pays no attention to them — because their father doesn't. Their absence confirms their father's inattention to his family.

That mystery also suggests an important element in this narrative. It does not purport to be a total vision of these characters' life. The story and the community are not completely detailed. Like some incidents left hanging, some plot details elliptical, these overlooked characters remind us that a world of life lies outside this story's frame. The family, Judaism, religion, Israel, all overflow this sampling of them. This is no invitation to speculate beyond the details we're given — just an acknowledgment that some reality was omitted as irrelevant.

This episode's most powerful plot line is Giti's heroic struggle to support her family yet keep Lippe's abdication secret. She insists he will return. She doesn't tell Ruchami that she's hunting for work. To protect Lippe she won't work in her neighbourhood. In a rare scene in the outside world, Giti trains out to a mall, hoping for a job. A businesswoman hires her to housekeep three days a week.

For that job Giti requires Ruchami to fill in at home, especially with infant Yehoshua. "This experience will help you in a few years when you're a mother," she says, rationalizing this imposition.

When Giti brings Ruchami a present the exhausted girl thanks her but immediately sets it aside, uninterested. The idea was more exciting than the gift. Then she confesses. Since they started to wean Yehoshua the formula has not satisfied him. Desperate to stop his crying, Ruchami reverted to nursing him. There is no milk there, it hurts her, but it stops his crying. "I'm not sure it's permitted."

Here religious dogma collides with compassion (in fact, what Ruchami's name connotes, the Hebrew *racham* or Yiddish *rachmonnis*). Must the regulatory brain overrule the instinctive heart? Giti recovers from her initial shock: "I'm not mad, Ruchami, but what you did was very bad. Don't do it again. Don't do it again. Ever."

It's a powerful scene. To help Giti, the young girl has had to act the mother. "Nursing" her infant brother is the ultimate extension of assuming her mother's responsibilities. Acknowledging this, after scolding her daughter Giti promotes her. "My little girl, my pet," she reassures her. Instead of more lying, she admits she doesn't know if

Lippe will return. Till then, Ruchami gets his bed in Giti's room, as if moving from child to parent.

But the religious ban must be respected, at whatever human cost. For it's all in God's hands. Alternatively: traceable back to Lippe's abandonment and Giti's determination to hide the truth. God is a convenient excuse for what we want to do or seek to approve.

Episode I,4

The first third of the season establishes, *inter alia*, Shulem's undermining his children. Having seen his damage to Giti and Akiva, we now learn how he stifled Zvi Arye. This past is revealed through a variety of phantoms.

In the opening scene, wife Tovi wakes him at 4 a.m. to deal with the phantom mouse she alone has seen and heard. Ever submitting to religious authority, Zvi Arye has been waiting for Rabbi Zimmerman to recommend an exterminator, or even summon "the mouse rabbi" Sihale. After catching his own finger in the trap, Zvi Arye takes matters in his own hands. He buys a pet mouse to produce as if he had trapped it. He can return it for a refund ("If the children don't like it").

His second phantom is frustrated ambition. Zvi Arye doesn't get the teaching job he wanted for a better salary. In despair, he flushes the mouse down the toilet. As he lost the refund, the mouse was presumably dead — a serious concern on the Facebook chatline — and consistent with the death of Zvi Arye's career hopes.

At Malka's 70th Anniversary party Zvi Arye suffers a ghost from his past. Uncle Nachum's 20-odd-year-old wedding video shows young Zvi Arye singing superbly. That pleases all but him. In one montage, the others laud the "wunderkind's" performance, but to Zvi Arye "It's nonsense." Akiva, in his own numb futility, pours himself a scotch, to Esti's concern. The celebration evokes dashed hopes.

Zvi Arye walks outside, where Shulem finds him crying. "A mouse catcher. I'm a mouse catcher.... I could have been a soloist. Performed all over the world." In I,i a TV concert reminded Malka wistfully of Zvi Arye's singing promise. He, Dvora, even the choir conductor wanted that career for him. Shulem forbade it. He forced his musical son into the yeshiva. As an emblem of dashed ardor, there's a fire extinguisher sign on the wall behind Zvi Arye as he weeps in his father's arms. Shulem makes no apology, shows no regret, acknowledges no responsibility for his son's misery. All is in God's hands.

Zvi Arye's name — which suggests the light gathering of a deer or gazelle — embodies the buoyant spirit a musical career might have given him, in contrast to his current heaviness.

As the next scene makes clear, Akiva has also compromised himself when he joined Leib Fuchs's "ghost painters." Esti is insightful: "You shouldn't have agreed. You're betraying your truth."

Akiva erupts: "Have you any idea what my truth is?" His truth would have him abandon Esti for Elisheva. But as at his proposal, Akiva is manipulated by Esti's crying. He apologizes for yelling, apologizes for having drunk too much, and agrees to call the next day.

Perhaps the episode's central theme is the compromises life imposes on our ambitions. This wisdom is placed in the mouth of the dishonest Fuchs: "If you want to make God laugh, tell Him your plans." Of course, Shulem not "life" thwarted Zvi Arye's musical ambition — or his own failure to challenge his father's and his community's authority, a formidable force indeed.

In other examples the characters work around their strictures. *Rebbitzin* Erblich, for example, has continued in the seniors' residence her husband's black market currency exchange business. She locks her cold cash in her fridge. When Giti learns of this she (i) catches the *rebbitzin*'s attempt to short-change her ("Even the rabbi made mistakes sometimes"), then (ii) negotiates to work for her at home on commission (negotiated from 50% down to 40). Giti stashes her cash in the family *Talmud*. "It's not 'dirty money,'" she tells the *rebbitzin*, "I earned it." In working within their strictures both women accept them.

In another practicality, employer Iris is pleased to see Giti's baby but tells her not to bring him to work again until she has clarified her insurance liability. With her new home income, Giti quits that job. Thus liberated, she tells Iris's young son that he really should make the blessing each time he eats or drinks something, a religious counsel from which she'd felt job-bound to exempt him.

Pragmatic adjustment is also the subject of the yeshiva debate we sample. The scholars explain how the sages have justified the ban against sailing anywhere within three days of the Sabbath. The reasons turn into metaphor: it's about crossing boundaries; it's related to the water being salty not sweet; it prevents any delay violating the Sabbath. The disparate purposes reduce the ban's authority. Zvi Arye does well — but it's not the success or life he craved.

So, too, Shulem's theological correction of his mother's hope to reunite with her dead husband. To discourage the anniversary party she wants him to organize, Shulem insists that in the afterlife men and women are still segregated. He did not make this point when Dvora wanted double burial spots for eternal togetherness (I,3). Indeed it is explicitly contradicted at the end of I, 12. Shulem's moral stories and theological arguments are usually false, biased towards his will.

Malka wisely drowns Shulem out by turning up the volume on the rock video. The forbidden TV has enlivened her. When Shoshanna describes her family's surprise 80th birthday party, Malka asks questions to help her visualize the scene better.

In a shadier pragmatism, the lads at Anshin's question the frequent fires at Idleman's pizzeria. But as Esti intuited, the shadiest is Akiva's new relationship with Leib Fuchs. "The painter?" Akiva asks. "The artist," Fuchs fallaciously corrects him. He's right to reject 'painter' — he can't paint. But his 'artist' is a Con.

When they meet on the bridge (an ominous crossing in Akiva's life), Fuchs is impressed enough by Akiva's drawings to invite him to his gallery to discuss a job. When Fuchs's granddaughter Hannah hands him his suitcase there is a playful allusion to the esteemed Holocaust survivor film, *Hana's Suitcase*. Treating this powerful emotional work so lightly here prepares us for the art Fuchs sells: schlock Judaica, largely old rabbi portraits and flowers.

Fuchs requires his "artists" to produce "copies" for him to sign and sell as his own. This is not art. He considers Akiva's painting of his grandparents too emotional. But when the Americans seeking "something with a Yiddish feel" want it, Fuchs overrides Akiva's refusal to sell — and pays him a bonus.

At Anshin's, Akiva uses his new income to toast this new stage in his life: he has a new bride, a new job, a new cell phone. But each is a compromise. It's not the woman he wants to marry, not the art he wants to make and the cell-phone is Esti's dad's castoff, a reminder of his unwanted connection.

Yet in the corrupt Fuchs's studio Akiva meets his first true artist. Sasha pays off his debts by doing Fuchs's hack work, but he makes his own art on the side. His expressionistic self-portrait is unlike anything Akiva has seen. In disdain Fuchs calls him "Rembrandt" — the master self-portraitist — and orders him to bring them drinks.

"When you work on your own painting," Sasha tells Akiva, "you'll paint from the heart." He assumes Akiva's pencil sketch of Elisheva is of his bride, for in this "special" portrait, the artist clearly loves his subject.

Akiva admits to Sasha that he hasn't gone to any art galleries outside synagogues. Going to one now makes him late to meet Esti for Malka's party. In this new world Akiva ignores Esti's phone call.

In the bridge scene Esti praised Akiva's drawing of ducks for its (a minor virtue) "accuracy." When she noted "They're closer together," he responds "I wasn't drawing them." Intuitively Akiva is already reaching beyond the representational in figurative art — an issue central to II,2. He's not recording that physical scene but reaching for its resonant signification. To Esti's credit, though she knows nothing about art her response to Akiva's "job" shows she grasps his ethical compromise. To the writers' credit, all the characters are allowed a mix of weakness and strength, virtue and folly. Thus the salty tears of her stratagem are balanced by the "honey" of Esti's name and manner.

Sasha's idealism extends beyond art. He is in love with his neighbour Ilana, who is not beautiful, whom he has never met, to whom he has never spoken, but to whose daily regimen of life he has become empathetically attuned. From her regular sounds, "My heart got used to her." "Day in, day out," by her daily sounds, he has been sharing her life. Sasha knows the woman he's never met better than Akiva knows his bride Esti.

Akiva picks up this emotion in the grandparents' photo he elects to paint: "The love of one day after another." Malka at her party repeats this wonder of quotidian love. At her husband's deathbed she forgot to mend the holes in his sweater. Now she has finally mended it. The sweater and the mending trigger her memories: "I forgot how happy we were all those years. What a privilege." But her happiness can't salve Zvi Arye's grief at and Akiva's resignation to aspirations dashed by their father's cruel authority.

Sasha's confession prompts Akiva to shoot a furtive cell-phone video of Elisheva coming home. This at least vicariously sustains a connection. In this drama's spectrum of art, Akiva's sentimental recording here aligns with the video of Nachum's wedding, the promised video of the Erblich birthday party, and the photo collection Akiva scans for his planned present to Malka. This recording of reality, art at its simplest, simply preserves experience to recall their attendant emotion. It's a respectable alternative to Fuchs's fraudulent copying of art. A more problematic "recording" artist, Aronofsky, appears in II,8.

The episode closes on Akiva's true feeling. In the night alley, amid the garbage, he finds light in his Elisheva video. The episode's last line is her resonant "Is anybody home?" Akiva wishes he were. To the sensitive, even a simple recording can rouse the emotions of art.

Episode I, 5

A new character carries this episode's central theme — the tension between self-assertion and submission in an oppressive culture. Shulem's brother-in-law Sucher is a 60-year-old bachelor who sells lottery tickets in a small booth in a distant square. Akiva suggests he move in with Shulem. But they didn't get along: "The only thing we had in common was that we both loved your mother."

Sucher's backstory is compelling. A yeshiva star student, he was engaged, then broke off the engagement, to the horror of the Haredim. While the jilted fiancee went on to prosper as a Mrs. Weinstein, now enjoying a grandchild's wedding, Sucher is a failure. When he invites Akiva in for tea, his cramped quarters are comic.

Sucher remains irreverent. Does he ever feel guilty for selling needy people the false hopes of a lottery win? No, he lets people leave a note hoping to have a prayer answered — just like the Wailing Wall.

Having left the Haredi community, Sucher wears a *kippah* but not the black suit and he has shorn his hair and sidelocks. He also joined the army, violating the sect's opposition to the Israeli military. When Shulem says Sucher screams in his sleep, we infer some kind of PTSD, whether from his war experience or his isolation. His scream ends the episode.

Akiva confides in Sucher his doubts over marrying Esti. He thinks Elisheva may love him despite rejecting him. Sucher replies that if he were Akiva he'd ask her. If she says Yes he'd [only!] think about it. But if she shows any doubt, he'd go through with the arranged marriage. That's if he were Akiva. "But if it's me I'd do nothing," *i.e.*, take the marriage. Sucher's assertion of his self proved too costly.

Akiva is detached from the inlaws' marriage planning. His only animation is seeing an old friend's name among the sample invitations. Otherwise, the discussion is dominated by his father's vanity. Shulem brushes off Gottlieb's preference for a modest wedding by ramping up the dinner. They'll have 400, then 500 and finally 520 dinners, allowing guests multiple entrees. This excess drives Akiva to the washroom.

In contrast to Akiva's reluctant submission, Shulem's respect for the norms is selfish. He angrily rejects Akiva's "Maybe rushing into marriage now isn't the right thing for me." It's natural for someone to feel doubts as the wedding approaches.

Shulem turns the heavy artillery of religious law against his son's right to a happy marriage. He lies: "The word 'doubt' in *gematria* is 'satan', or something like that." It's not. The learned Shulem equates Satan with Amalek, the letters of whose name is the same as the *gematria* value of the letters for "doubt."[7] This misrepresents a dubiously pertinent text. Shulem asserts that everything holy is certain; the devil undermines it with irrational cynicism. But doubting Esti is not the same as doubting God.

Shulem won't be doubted. He gleefully exploits the funeral proclamation outside to claim divine support for Akiva's wedding. Rabbi Cheshin's death means Akiva can have his job — to support marriage to Esti. This is a sign from God — that Akiva should marry the woman he doesn't love. "Wondrous are the ways of the Lord." Shulem uses religion against his son's well-being.

Despite his ostensible dedication to religious values, for Shulem any relationship centers on food. It's the only nourishment he seeks. Hence his opening line: "It's worth getting married for the Waldorf salad." For his Waldorf he would sacrifice his son at the altar.

Shulem visits Aliza for her food. He dismisses her suggestion of a union, even though she's unhappy living alone: "Live alone, die alone.... At least you come here to eat." At his bristling she retreats: "I

---

[7] I thank Elana Horwitz for this explanation.

like having you eat here." When she mentions possibly meeting a rich divorced American, Shulem loses his chance: "I'm happy for you."

Shulem's narrow "appetite" for marriage makes the Akiva-Elisheva romance even more touching. In her uncertainty Elisheva revisits her two dead husbands (eating). Israel (after whom their son is named) criticizes her for a late ("orphan") ritual Amen and for wearing a dress that would attract the bus driver's compliment. She responds with the familiar charge against male authority: "Stop educating me as if I'm a little girl. It's your fault I have to raise Israel alone.... It's your fault I had to give up a good match." They say "There's room for one more."

Akiva's lingering love for Elisheva is imaged in his warming himself at the heater she returned. As Sucher advised, he phones her: "Tell me outright that you feel nothing for me." She says nothing but lets him come see her. She respects the proprieties they are violating when, as a betrothed man, he phones her and he asks to visit. He must leave the door ajar when he enters.

Then she commits a dramatic impropriety — to persuade him to forget her. In the most erotic scene in the entire series, she removes her wig and unfurls her flowing black hair. She leans forward to show him its beginning traces of grey.

"You're so young You look at me with those innocent eyes.... You're caught in a fantasy of me," she says. He sees only the beauty she used to be. Finally, "I can't do this.... I can't start over again. Love. A wedding. Furniture.... Another life. I just can't do it." She sends him away: "Marry your bride. Forget about me." On her final "Goodbye, Akiva" she turns away from him and cries. Unlike Esti, in non-manipulative silence.

Akiva's banishment segues into Shulem's. When he comes to Aliza for dinner there is no response. At school she reports that she has met the American. That nice serious man, pointedly, "knows what he wants." Shulem criticizes her for acting on his denial of romantic interest: "If I told you to jump off a roof would you jump off a roof?" He retreats: "Take care, Aliza. Good luck to you."

Now driven to feed himself, Shulem stocks up on noodle boxes, resenting the cost for non-MSG. So he courts Rabbi Cheshin's widow, Edna. He gives her the expensive Stollen cake, baked in early winter but expected to age slowly into maturity — like a courtship.

The pattern on the neckline of Edna's dress dooms his chances. It's an image of straps with a clasp at the top, suggesting her containment, enclosure, self-sufficiency. In a society where women dress plainly, this emblem is eloquent —another reminder of this drama's attention to expressive detail.

In the opening scene Gottlieb's embrace of Akiva carries the seeds of their division. He thanks Akiva for bringing happiness to the favourite of his eight offspring. "When my daughter's happy I'm happy." He urges Akiva to call him father. "You can give me a strong handshake. [But his fist engulfs Akiva's] Don't be shy."

The doting dad's dedication to his "princess" gives Akiva his way out. As the fathers write the wedding cheques Gottlieb reports that he had to pay an extra $250 to get The Yeshiva Boys band to cancel another engagement. Shulem volunteers to help on that charge. But Akiva picks up on the father's remark that Esti cried relentlessly when she couldn't have *that* band. "My wife says I melt when she cries, and I do." Akiva remarks that Esti's crying changed his mind from ending their relationship to marrying her.

In ruling by tears, Esti proves as selfish and manipulative as Shulem. But we can feel for her. Lacking the power of male authority, she deploys her weakness. Though Akiva is blamed, Gottlieb ends the engagement: "My daughter is no man's consolation prize. I should have listened to my wife. She said Akiva is too peculiar."

The engagement crumbles despite Shulem's lies about Akiva's true feelings and his demand his son repent. Again, Shulem is more selfish than principled: "Start digging my grave." His embarrassment not Akiva's happiness is his ruling issue.

In revenge Shulem throws out Akiva's bedding and (Elisheva's returned) heater, banishing him. Akiva retreats to Sucher's. When he returns home Shulem, ever self-unaware, is surprised to find Akiva gone. Between those who follow their honest impulses and those who submit to repressive orders, Sucher's scream speaks for them all.

Episode I, 6

At breakfast with Akiva the morning after that scream, Sucher hides behind the cereal box. He apologizes that having lived alone so long, he can't stand being with people. In a more solitary breakfast Shulem toys with his unbuttered bread. The butter is unthawed. In familial contrast, Ruchami spreads cream cheese for her brothers' lunch.

At the season's halfway point this episode details solitudes and reunions. When Lippe phones from Argentina Ruchami hangs up on him. Giti tries to curb her daughter's rage: "I know that in your heart you pray for his return. As I do." Ruchami's anger is a measure of her devotion to her father, that he radically betrayed. When they part in I,1 she tells him "I miss you already."

As she assumes more home responsibilities, Ruchami proves a precocious reader. It has fired her imagination. In I,2 she whimsically suggests that Lippe may have disappeared while flying into the Bermuda Triangle. Censorship at the library forces librarian Yuta to hide significant literature in a secret "stash" for Ruchami. Those all read, she'll now bring some from her home. The contraband includes George Eliot's *Middlemarch* and *"Hannah" Karenina*, the Tolstoy that Ruchami reads sanitized to her brothers at bedtime.

Why those titles? Dorothea and Anna are both strong-willed, intense heroines that would inspire a young girl growing up. This outsider literature poses an intriguing question: Will she read them within the framework of her religious community or will they lead her to break out? In either case, her mature reading prepares the girl who initiates her own marriage in the second season.

It works already. On the librarian's computer Ruchami writes letters to her brothers, supposedly from their absent father. This is "creative" writing however functional. The cross-gender writing derives from "George Eliot." After "he" specifically invites 12-year-old Yosa'le to write what's closest in his heart, the boy confesses his bedwetting. Ruchami addresses his shame, explains the normalcy and proposes solutions. Having filled in for their mother, Ruchami now fills in for the dad. She writes "his" letters to each boy but none to herself: "I'm a big girl. I can get over the longing." That she has.

In assuming her father's "voice" or role here, Ruchami takes another step into maturity. Along with the forbidden literature Ruchami adopts Yuta's fake cigarette, paralleling the men's snuff. Also, she performs a more legitimate version of her forbidden mothering, when she "nursed" her infant brother to still his crying. Apparently Jewish law does not forbid giving advice. In Shira Haas's performance — a gem among gems — we often catch Ruchami quietly watching, hearing, responding, a young person of sentience, judgement and courage. Defending her uncle, she tells Shoshanna that stories of Akiva's breaking his engagement are "slander." Ruchami stands alone on that truth.

Meanwhile, Shulem sticks to Akiva's banishment, changing the locks, ignoring his son's teachers room plea to be allowed home, turning his back on his knocking. Zvi Arye invites Akiva to stay but condemns him for shaming the family: "Jewish law says better to get married and divorced than break off the engagement.... You only care for yourself, like a little boy." When Zvi Arye tries to reconcile his father and brother, Shulem diminishes him too: "Don't be so humble. You're not that important." Projecting his own guilt, Shulem falsely accuses Sucher of kicking out Akiva.

When his friends and Anshin can't accommodate him Akiva takes a cabbie's advice and turns to the spare room in the synagogue basement. A cabbie? Such is the advantage of a tight community. There Akiva befriends the German caretaker Oliver, a large man the congregants call The Golem, who over a beer lets him stay. Oliver is impressed by Akiva's pencil portrait of him: "You're a real artist." He asks Akiva what "Golem" means. No, Akiva assures him, it doesn't mean "idiot." It's a fictional medieval Prague character made of mud to help the Jews. As Oliver does. The two outcasts comfort each other.

The opening montage of breakfast scenes is echoed in a series of Sabbath celebrations. In the first Lippe has called Giti to say he wants to return but he needs two more months to grow back his beard and sidelocks. His shearing is as troubling as his infidelity. A cross on the wall confirms how far his adventure has taken him. It supports the rumour he ran off with a Gentile. Even if he didn't hang it, it defines his present space, the extent of his alienation. Then Giti lights her *shabbes* candles.

Akiva leads a Sabbath celebration with Oliver, over wine, candle and blessings. Unlike Lippe, even on his own Akiva keeps up his religion. In contrast, Shulem sits alone over his Sabbath dinner, singing about the inestimable value of a good wife. (His Sabbath isolation will be painfully amplified in his last scene in Season Two.)

This leads to Shulem's climactic recollection of Dvora in Akiva's boyhood. More specifically: Shulem's undermining Dvora's bonds with her son. As Dvora says, men have no idea of a mother's experience. Hence the patriarch's belligerent insecurity. Shulem tells the new yeshiva student Akiva to call home only once a week, before the Sabbath: "His soul won't be elevated if he's always calling his mother." Shulem disconnects the phone every night, then assures Dvora the boy's not calling home is "a good sign."

Shulem more seriously restricts his son's experience by endangering his vision, again restricting his experience putatively to elevate his soul. So he won't see women on the bus Shulem put his own glasses on Akiva to blur his vision. Despite the resultant headache, he assures the boy that bad glasses don't ruin the eyesight. Looking at things you shouldn't look at does. Religion overrules optometry. "Control your eyes so they won't control you." To the patriarch every issue is a battle for control.

Little Akiva fakes a vision problem to get glasses that would obscure his sight of women. The optometrist concludes "Your son may be confused but he doesn't need glasses." Where blinkers restrict vision, the wrong glasses distort what one sees with physiological danger. Shulem's threat to his son's vision typifies his harmful control.

When Dvora confronts him Shulem says it's "odd" that the boy lied about his sight. And they didn't hear the phone ring: "We'll get a louder phone." Seeing through Shulem's lies, Dvora yells "Shame on you!" He admits to disconnecting the phone — "But I didn't tell him to lie!" Furiously Dvora pounds Shulem with all she has, a pillow. As a weapon that's little better than Esti's tears.

Chastened by this memory, Shulem descends to the synagogue furnace room to invite Akiva back. He finds him playing chess with Oliver. With his usual insensitivity, Shulem cites Oliver's demeaning nickname when he asks Akiva "Why are you standing there like a Golem?" Shulem doesn't apologize to Akiva for ejecting him, nor admit either to an error or to a change of heart. He ordered too much food from Anshin and doesn't want to waste it. Again Shulem's sense of a relationship pivots on food. His selfishness fails to nourish anyone else.

Of the two sensory deprivations Shulem recalls here the visual is the more significant. As Akiva grows into an artist he overcomes the restrictions Shulem tried to place on his sight. The second season conclusion pivots on Shulem's distorted vision of an Akiva painting and his violation of Dvora's values in his ostensible defence of them.

Like the season's opening and closing scenes, its first half closes on a dream. Ruchami's dream more than Giti's hope reveals what her heart feels for her unfaithful father. The western Ruchami glimpsed in her grandmother's TV prompts her dream of a showdown with Lippe. "Do something!" she repeats. As his only response is laughing, she shoots him down like the varmint he is. The medium and the genre represent the culture this sect rejects — and the license for which Lippe abandoned his family. But like Shulem's restriction of Akiva's vision and the library censorship, a forbidden reality persists.

Episode I, 7

The episode's central symbol is the planetary model that Shulem uses to explain the imminent solar eclipse. His enthusiasm for science is surprising, for it offers a secular alternative to the religious heaven. The model serves two larger points, one which Shulem uses on Akiva and one in which Shulem is himself exposed.

In the first, Shulem encourages Akiva to resume courting Elisheva. "Now that you've ruined your reputation and you're second-hand goods," he says supportively, "go ahead." To address Elisheva's reluctance, Shulem draws an astronomical parallel: "Things move on earth as they do in the sky…. The sun must be stable for the planets to revolve around…. You have to stand firm like the sun… and she will start to revolve around you." Like the wedding dance, he adds. If the man asserts his natural authority the woman will move around him, dependent upon his strength and warmth. Should the man or sun waver — chaos.

That's patriarchy. The man assumes he is the sun-like centre of his family universe, with divinely bestowed authority. Against Akiva's qualms Shulem insists "Times change but the Jew remains the same. The sun remains the same."

The second and contrary lesson of that solar model is that perception changes with perspective. "This is what we look like from there" he says, pointing to the miniature Earth. When a student remarks "Rabbi, you look just like God," Shulem fakes humility: "You mustn't say that. Your rabbi is merely flesh and blood."

That mortality leads to a new perspective that shakes Shulem's vanity. His paycheck has been halved. When Principal Wasserstein's excuse of general salary reductions proves untrue, Shulem leads his pupils into a sit-in outside Wasserstein's office, on the pertinent Psalm 130, *The Song of Ascents*: "Out of the depths I raise my voice, the voice of my supplication." Again Shulem proffers a personal position as religion.

Wasserstein's news sinks Shulem further. He'd had to retire at 60. But Dvora came to Wasserstein's home to plead for his extension. Malka provided postdated cheques to cover the difference between Shulem's pension and his salary. Dvora feared Shulem might die upon retirement, as his father did. As the cheques have run out, Shulem can stay as volunteer or — the time has come ?— retire.

The news shatters Shulem's confidence. He feels misled and betrayed, "like a child." "I've never felt so foolish in my life. All this time I thought I'm a strong man. It turns out it was all a play" (The word '*shpiel*' is in the subtitles mistranslated as 'circus').

Worse, Shulem's authority was based on two women propping him up. "Industrious" Dvora begged Principal Wasserstein for the ruse and "queen" Malka paid for it. Confronting Malka, Shulem vents his anger at Dvora for having deceived him. His anger hides his embarrassment that his wife and mother were the true source of his presumed strength. So much for the sun animating the planets.

In the bank, news of his overdrawn account adds to the shock of his retirement. Again a woman senses his weakness and comes to help: Elisheva recognizes him and brings him a glass of water.

Nor is Principal Wasserstein a model male authority. Having humanely obliged the women he fails to act promptly, to let Malka renew the checks. Confronted by Shulem, he evades the issue by lying, fearing to confront him with the truth. For the male head of the male school, Wasserstein proves weak and ineffectual.

As the school watches the solar eclipse Akiva notices Shulem wearily carting his personal belongings away from the school. Thinking he was the center of his world, he discovers himself marginalized. The family sun is eclipsed. The closing shot is of Akiva's sympathetic concern for his father, not that reduction.

As Shulem weakens, Giti discovers a new strength. Purely with her anger she drives off a man who tries to rob her at knifepoint. Her crowning insult — "I hope they cut your beard off, you vile man" — anticipates Lippe delaying his return until his beard's back. Giti declines his offer to return earlier, to help him save face.

To protect his own image Shulem encourages Giti to quit her currency exchange. He's concerned for her safety, but "it looks bad." With a bank loan he gives her 10,000 shekels, urging her to quit "at least till Lippe returns." She declines his money: "I'm a big girl.... I have it under control." She insists he not tell Lippe.

Incidentally, Shulem's claim to be paying six mortgages may be another lie. He is unlikely to be paying for his Chabad outcast, or even for his mother's long-owned flat, in which Zvi Arye lives free, or even for his own, where he has lived for decades. Shulem may view each child as a mortgage. Or a planet dependent upon his support.

Like Shulem's, Lippe's swagger rings hollow: "I'd show [the thief] if I were home. I'd kill him." Yet Giti ends their phone chat on her vulnerability, not strength. "I don't want to be a hero," she says, "or an object of pity." She needs him to return, to stand beside her at the family center. This differs from the husband as sole sun/center. Giti makes Lippe listen to her cry, both for her emotional release and for him to realize his responsibility. Ruchami overhears this with gathering anger at her father but also — *pace* Season Two — with a growing sense of a wife's responsibility and strength.

In lighter shifts of perspective, there is a parody of rabbinical seriousness when Giti's two older sons play at flipping cards bearing famous rabbis' images. So, too, artist Fuchs's brazen commercializing of religious "art." He can paint anything, even "The Messiah. I can't bring him but I can paint him for you."

In a comic play on self-perception, Fuchs asks Akiva to paint Fuchs's self-portrait, in the tradition of all the great artists' self-portraits. They usually did their own. Akiva starts the assignment to his radio's religious rock ballad: "Wake up in the morning, Wake up in my yearning…. Can you hear me, Lord? Save me from myself." Fuchs's idea of a self-portrait is to avoid himself, specifically his own shallowness and his inability to paint.

The Fuchs photo is so fatuous Akiva adds lipstick and a red nose to the painting. As he browses through the book of self-portraits Akiva intuits the essence of the genre. Where Fuchs's eyes ring hollow, the great self-portraits catch the artist focused on the depths of the human condition, mortality, "looking into himself." He asks to shoot Fuchs being introspective, serious, but the ersatz artist recoils from Akiva's prompting: "Think about the mistakes you made in your life…. the loves… your fears and failures." The "artist" flees that foray into his self.

Now Akiva ventures into the proper self-portrait, probing his own emotion. Giving it to Elishiva clearly affects her. Her response to Akiva's self-exposure builds on her earlier interest, when she asked Israel about his teacher's mood and mien.

Episode I, 8

Continuing the theme of self-portraiture, the shadows of death and loss fall across this episode. First, Shulem has a heart issue while visiting Edna, Rabbi Cheshin's widow. As the doctor requires him to monitor his activity, for recording and analysis, Shulem acknowledges his mortality. He turns generous, buying Zvi Arye "on sale" potatoes and talking to his grandchildren.

With Edna Shulem slips into his old exploitation of Aliza. He even orders up dishes she hasn't made before. Yet he bristles at Edna's care, fearing to appear dependent. He's indignant when she assumes he might be at loose ends upon retirement, as her husband was — and as Dvora had feared (I,7). As Shulem is rolled into the CT scan Edna calls him Eleazar, her late husband's name,.

The old meets the new when Shulem has electrodes planted under his undergarment *tallis kotton*. He enters the scanner praying *Shema Yisroel*. Fearing weakness, he's touchy when Akiva comes home having eaten out: "We should rent out the kitchen?"

Giti is having an inside camera installed when Shulem phones. "How is Lippe?" he asks, as if newly aware of his responsibility for his son-in-law's absence. "Is he mad at me?" No, she replies: "That's all in the past. It was for the best." She responds as if Lippe had already returned. Abed, Shulem prays "Grant me light so I do not sleep the sleep of death." He prays to awaken, not to be illuminated.

Akiva and Elisheva continue their dance. In the bank he proposes they meet by chance at his friend Levi Itzhak's klezmer band performance. As going together would be inappropriate they would go separately and sit apart. Besides, the club is not frequented by "the ultra-ultra-orthodox," as Akiva if not Elisheva identifies.

As she eagerly prepares to go, Elisheva is dissuaded by son Israel's innocent questioning: "Where are you going?... To meet a man?... Like when you date? To get married?" Elisheva squirms away from his help with her necklace, then decides not to go. Again, her motherhood deters her romance.

 In an enigmatic, touching plot extension, Akiva coaxes the reluctant Levi Itzhak first to seek out, then to meet, his lost mother, who apparently gave him up for adoption. Levi Itzhak is reluctant to find her: "Can she restore things the way they were?" Akiva persists "Because you're my friend. Because I can no longer meet my mother" — except in his "silly dreams." In exchange for Levi Itzhak seeking her out, Akiva agreed to ask out Elisheva again. In exchange for meeting the woman, Akiva agrees to a Sabbath camping trip with him at Hokuk beach on Lake Kinneret.

The men's ploy to meet the woman is to solicit donations to a charity for orphans (!). Akiva asks for a bite to eat, as they've been on their feet all day. Over dinner Levi Itzhak watches his mother, her older son and young grandson. Levi Itzhak grows disturbed. On the bus he retreats to silence, but not out of anger at Akiva: "This whole thing is exhausting." The next day, after Akiva buys the food for their retreat, he hears that Levi Itzhak cried all night and finally signed himself into the psychiatric hospital.

This surprising tangent is the only drama outside the Shtisel family. In the forest scene (I,3) Levi Itzhak quoted Kierkegaard's resignation to unhappiness. Learned but lighthearted, he seemed one of the more substantial of Akiva's yeshiva pals. He's visibly more secular, in his appearance and his Sabbath camping trips, so he hasn't drawn as fully on the Haredi community. He never knew his mother.

Yet in his band he provides the core, the bass. One passing image catches the difficult balance in faith, humanity and life: two men dance together, each balancing a bottle on his head. This counters the men's slippery footing motif in I,3.

In the club Levi Itzhak sings a Yiddish song by the cantor Pinchas Segal. In the song — "about food and people" —the sages have declared there are three kinds of people. But they prove to be all the same. In all cases, the men come home from the synagogue and ask their wife if she has prepared (i) a borscht, or (ii) meat, and in the omitted verse (iii) presumably some other vittle. Whether the wife replies Yes or No the man's response is the same: *"Nu? Nu?"* "So? So?" A common stoicism underlies these supposed differentiations. Whatever our expectations, however they're resolved, we carry on. But not in Levi Itzhak's experience here.

Perhaps this song and the Levi Itzhak tangent evoke a Tolstoy quote rather than Kierkegaard: "All happy families are alike; each unhappy family is unhappy in its own way." That opens Ruchami's *Anna Karenina*. The bassist sings a happy front but he lives a tragedy. His solitude is as stultifying as a suppressive family can be. Yet for all this pathos, the song is a light-hearted version both of Kierkegaard's resignation to unhappiness and of Shulem basing his relationships on food.

As for that *Nu? Nu?*: In I,7 Fuchs defined the homonymous *nudnik*: "He's the man who, when you say 'How are you?' he tells you." Levi Itzhak's breakdown, for all his light-hearted spirit, is an understandable response to glimpsing his unknown mother's life, the life that he might have inhabited, the support he might have enjoyed.

In the Shtisel family tangle, this story reminds us that finding a lost mother can be as painful as losing a known one. A missing parent can be as problematic as an oppressive one. At dinner Levi Itzhak glimpses the life he might have had. Without the grounding of even a problematic parent, he crumbles.

Not allowed to visit Levi Itzhak, Akiva leaves the Sabbath food for him at the desk, hoping it will be passed on. As he leaves, he pauses at his mother's grave. There he draws more strength from his dead mother than his friend can from his living one. Over Akiva's approach to her grave we hear Shulem addressing his will to his children: "I feel my time is approaching." He wants to be buried beside his Dvora.

Having funded each other child's apartment purchase (but not Zvi Arye's!), he now bequeaths his own to Akiva — but only after he has been married for a year. Dvora's emotional legacy to Akiva clearly surpasses Shulem's material one.

Then Shulem's voice segues into cantor Segal's recording of Levi Itzhak's earlier song, *Nu? Nu?* The cantorial heft and ardor are more intense than the club rendition. It is more wail than play. The difference in the music matches the difference between Akiva's and his friend's emotional nourishment. However problematic a family — or a community — it can provide a support the isolated don't know.

As the season's one-third mark revealed Shulem's damage to Zvi Arye, the two-thirds episode reveals another family's dissolution and Shulem's late attempt to correct his failures as a father.

Episode I,9

The first two shots are opposing profiles of Akiva. The two are one. This episode focuses on identity — individual and religious.

Akiva's melancholy visit with Levi Itzhak in the psychiatric hospital still manages a joke: the orderly summons Akiva to the group counselling session. "No, I'm the patient," Levi Itzhak asserts. On one level the error is right because Akiva is — as Zvi Arye remarks — "troubled all the time." In a culture of suppression Akiva expresses emotions. The orderly's mistake shows the uncertainty of an identity.

Attorney Zeybart offers a metaphysical version of this theme in his joke about the two rabbis. One claims to be the Messiah, appointed by God. The other claims to be God — and denies appointing him. Who's the inmate, who the visitor? How firm is one's identity?

On the family level, we first hear of Shulem's daughter Racheli when she sues him before the rabbincal court to "uphold his duty as father and grandfather." He must resume his lapsed identity. As a child Racheli "had a mouth on her, but to the proper extent." Her feistiness hardened when she became "a messianic Chabadnik with all the trimmings." She married another messianic Chabadnik — a Sephardic, to boot — then disappeared into Nahariya. That's her changed identity.

Shulem assumes her lawsuit is for money. He asks Akiva to call her, to tell her to back off, but Akiva demurs. Shulem makes Akiva go with him to see her.

His daughter only wants him to appear once a week to teach his three young grandsons. That's his inclination anyway. When Racheli comes home she finds Shulem giving the boys a Biblical quiz — with impressive results. Their Chabad upbringing has not left them ignorant pagans! Typically, Shulem later negotiates her down to one visit every two weeks — when he can manage it. Shulem limits his parental responsibilities far more than his authority.

Shulem's identity is an issue *chez* Baruch. The kids have been told Bubba Dvora's husband died many years ago. Her portrait hangs on the wall, with another old man where Shulem's would be. Clearly Racheli broke more harshly from Shulem than from Dvora, as yeshiva-bound Akiva did. Carefully, Shulem greets Racheli with a formal "Hello lady of the house," rather than "daughter."

A surreal confusion of identity involves the "baby" that Zvi Arye and Tovi discover in a coffin-like box in Malka's attic. The "baby" is a small 100-year-old Torah dedicated to honour the Shulem, son of Velvale, after whom our Shulem, son of Velvale, was named.

The confusion is calculated. Tovi is shocked to read "Baby" on the box. "You found the baby in the attic?" Zeybart overhears. On the train to Nahariya the woman Adi takes the "baby" swaddled in a prayer shawl to be human, especially when the men panic at almost dropping it. She suggests they uncover the sleeping baby's face. When the "baby" is explained she asks to kiss the Torah. Adi is new to her faith: "Six months ago I started to find my religion." The sentiment of the "baby" draws her to it, with the passion of the recent "convert."

Shulem uses the baby Torah as a pretext to visit his daughter, as if he were not responding to her lawsuit: "I'm here as a customer," bringing the Torah to be repaired by her scribe husband. Again he uses religion for his personal purpose, to save face in reconnecting with his daughter.

After his heart issue, Shulem takes the discovery of his namesake's Torah to be a divine sign that his "time is up." So "All I want is to be beyond reproach when I ascend to the Heavenly Court." "Are you asking for forgiveness?" his daughter asks. "I'm asking for forgiveness. Absolutely." Whether from her or from God is left unsaid.

When husband Eran declares the Torah beyond repair, the three drive out to bury it. *En route* Shulem has his second dream of his Final Judgment.

In the first dream, attorney Zeybart is also an officer of the Heavenly Court. Though he considered Shulem safe from the lawsuit on earth, "Up here they know the truth and the truth is you're a piece of *dreck*" (excrement). Nor do we escape our vulnerabilities in heaven. We can still have heart attacks (some Jews have 10 or 12 a day).

In his second dream, Shulem finds himself behind Eran at the entrance to the Heavenly Court. Eran is there for Shulem. "May I call you Father?" "Of course," Shulem says, then asks Eran to explain what's happening. They are waiting to appear before The Rabbi, who has a wad of cash. "If you get a dollar you go straight to Heaven. If you don't, God help you." Even Shulem conceives of Heaven in earthly terms.

Shulem worries about the proliferation of Jewish identities thus competing for Heaven: "That's unfair. Do you know how many Lithuanian Jews there are? How many Satmers? How many kosher Jews who don't believe in The Rabbi? Is He going to send them all to Hell?"

No, Eran assures him, The Rabbi loves all the Jews. "He even loves the gentiles." In a new openness Shulem gratefully accepts Eran's Chabad banner: "Prepare yourself for the Messiah."

Here the differences that Jews — and by Eran's extension, gentiles — assert between themselves are insignificant to God. Issues of humanity trump the differentiations by which various faiths define themselves. This replays the drama's central theme: valuing compassion over religious conventions. In this ecumenical spirit, calling that Torah a baby evokes the Word becoming Flesh in Christianity. That is one loaded metaphor.

Despite his fear of final judgment, twice Shulem reveals his mean spirit. First, he is excessively affronted by Zvi Arye's joke: instead of donating the little Torah to the synagogue now, perhaps he and Akiva could keep it to donate in honour of Shulem's death. "We won't even have to change the cover." Shulem bristles: "A Jew brings children into this world and all they do is cause him grief." He may have Racheli's revolt in mind as well as Zvi Arye's (not bad) quip.

Shulem's seriousness about mortality is arbitrary. He himself joked black after intruding upon Akiva's phone call to Elisheva: "Soon you'll have 50 years of privacy." Upset by Shulem's anger, Zvi Arye delivers an abject apology — that Shulem is too self-obsessed to hear.

Shulem's second coldness is on the train. While Akiva is open to chatting with the friendly stranger Adi, Shulem dismisses her: "May your soul be elevated as you serve God." When Akiva calls him on this rudeness Shulem insists "It hurts me to see you waste your time on confused women and on books that don't befit a Jew." Despite that rudeness Adi drives Shulem to Racheli's home. A graphic designer, she gives him her card, in case he may need her help again. He will. In the next episode he's humiliated by exposing *his* confusion and vanity.

In a parallel "kindness of strangers"[8] Akiva, who left his money in his jacket when he escaped Shulem on the train at Acre, gets an expensive cab ride to the Hokuk beach in exchange for painting a bright mural in the cabbie's nursery. The colourful forest scene amplifies the black and white sketch Akiva drew in his classroom. This is art freed from restraint, however commissioned.

The episode ends with Akiva and Shulem both in moments approximating to Christian grace. Of course: separately.

Akiva finds himself on the beach to which Levi Itzhak planned to take him. Akiva was frustrated earlier when Shulem interrupted his serious call to Elisheva, then again by his forced train-ride. Now he strolls among the secular celebrants in their colourful and revealing beachwear, rolls up his pant-legs and wades into the sea. One shot dissolves into the next, as if to embody his softening. In our last sight of Akiva he floats serenely in the sea, at rare peace with himself and the world. As the dream Eran expressed the equivalence of all religions in God's eye, Akiva's peace in the water evokes baptism.

After burying the baby Torah Shulem is also at a new peace, not least with his daughter. He doubts his old authority: "You think you've got it all figured out, but then you find you don't understand a thing." He glances at the water behind them, but doesn't enjoy Akiva's immersion.

---

[8] Not here, Blanche du Bois from *A Streetcar Named Desire*.

We last see Shulem on the train dangling a happy baby on his lap. This openness goes beyond his rare friendliness towards Zvi Arye's children (I,8). His enjoyment of this stranger's baby also contrasts to his dismissal of Adi. The ritual baby Torah gives way to a live baby — a familiar representation of the messiah in that well-known Jewish offshoot, Christianity. Like Akiva's figurative baptism, Shulem's hopeful infant transcends religious differences. The Christian imagery closes this episode on the note of renewal, rebirth, anticipating Shulem's recovery from bis heart ailment by the next episode.

Episode I, 10

This episode begins in Shulem's strutting vanity and ends in Akiva's intimacy, a clear advance. Shulem spends big shekels on a Brandolino high hat ("no discount"), indeed 1,850 shekels on wardrobe. He excuses this extravagance: "I just got my life back." His heart has been cleared, at least medically. Chastened by fear of death, he responds to his rebirth with a pathetic swagger.

The episode closes on Akiva making a breakfast omelet for Elisheva in her kitchen. Unlike Shulem, Akiva cooks for his lady. While his father moves through futile romantic attempts Akiva focuses on her. He persuades her to become engaged without committing to marriage, so they can be together more freely.

"Can't a Jew dress nicely?" — Shulem excuses his lavish wardrobe. In Edna's photo, the egotist Shulem notices only her husband's Brandolino. She declines his invitation to a walk and dinner, preferring to work on the family photo album. "I'm not the adventurous type," she explains. "I'm moving on," Shulem responds. "By the way, this is a Brandolino." She remains unimpressed.

Shulem is next thwarted when secretary Aliza reveals she is now Mrs Gerlick. Having accepted her tea he now rejects her biscuits. He asks Konigsberg to find him a match: "I want a woman with some spirit, with verve, not an old bag." Then, magnanimously: "She can be younger than me." When the matchmaker proposes Edna, Shulem ends the commission, to hunt on his own.

Blinded by his vanity, Shulem makes a date with Adi, the young woman on the train. On the phone he pretends he doesn't know whose number he dialled. The date arranged, Shulem warns Akiva:

"Who knows? You might not be my youngest forever." He explains his fancy new duds: "They're all I could find." He claims Konigsberg insisted on setting up the meeting. The date starts in lies and ends on inexorable truth.

When they meet, Adi confuses the names Shulem and Shalom. She hoped he was proposing a match with Akiva. She won't marry a man "60, give or take," as she is only 37. At their son's bar mitzvah the father would be 75. Embarrassed to learn Shulem was proposing himself, she salves his ego with compliments: "I wish you could be my rabbi, my father even." Humiliated, Shulem rejects her suggestion they talk awhile anyway. "Loser, idiot, bum," he fumes at himself, tossing his proud Brandolino in the dumpster. "No harm done," he repeats, to deny his humiliation. His sexual presumption reflects the power a patriarchy grants men.

Subbing in Akiva's class, Shulem sets the *Gemarah* aside to tell the boys a frightening story about "The White Man." This mysterious character from old Jerusalem was named for his all-white wardrobe. We don't know what horror ensues or its promised "moral." The story could respond to the failure of Shulem's expensive black clothing to have empowered him with Adi.

Hungry for some success, Shulem has Aliza tell the board he's willing to become the new principal. Wasserstein was just fired for introducing secular studies (against Shulem's counsel, he claims) — presumably beyond an astronomy lesson. Shulem's romantic failure drives him back to the insularity where he'd enjoyed success.

Akiva's romantic progress begins when he is hit by an American tourist's car. Coincidentally, when Elisheva hears that a young man was killed in such a collision she intuitively worries for Akiva. He argues that the coincidental accidents prove they should wed. Though relieved to see him alive, she still rejects his suit. "I'm alive, Elisheva, and you're alive. Perhaps you only love dead people." When he comes to apologize, she lets him in to say his morning prayers while she goes for groceries.

The revival of Akiva's hopes is paralleled by another resurrection — his treasured painting of his grandparents. Fuchs has it back from the buyers, to whom "Something happened and they had to go back to America." One of the car accidents, perhaps. The Lord moves in mysterious ways. Fuchs offers to sell it to Akiva, who bargains him down. "You're quite a hustler," Fuchs says, respectfully.

Notably, we don't see the painting again after this episode. Nor do we see the self-portrait Akiva gave Elisheva. Two points may be at work here. One, for all our emotional investment both in the making of and the engagement with art, a painting is just a thing, of no greater heft or value than the rest of our brief gossamer existence on earth, not to mention in fiction. So, too, Shulem's last scene in Season Two.

Secondly, both paintings in question here are like the other loose ends left dangling, like *tsitsis* on the prayer shawl. After the intense drama of Levi Yitzhak, we don't see him or his mother again, nor hear of any consequences to his breakdown (except for two subtle allusions, later). As with Shulem's mysterious two extra children, we're reminded that life goes on outside the frame that this story establishes, with what's irrelevant to its themes therefore excluded.

However detailed we find these characters' lives, however fully realized their personalities, this drama doesn't purport to comprehensiveness. The society it details is not a tightly framed summary of human existence, not even of the religious disposition. Other lives, other dramas, other faiths, other institutions continue beyond it, of equal reality. Its interest lies in what it reflects beyond itself without being comprehensive. Though nothing outside the narrative is pertinent to our reading of it, its complete self-containment provides a sample not the total life it approaches.

Between the two Shtisel men's romantic campaigns, Giti prepares for Lippe's return. In her first shot she's pounding some frozen chicken to prepare for their *shabbes* thaw. She tries to warm Ruchami out of hating her father: "We'll be a normal family again." But Ruchami is unforgiving: "Why should I give up my bed for him? He can sleep in the street with his *shicksa.*"

While Ruchami sews a yellow star on her blouse for the school's Holocaust play, a street crier outside summons the citizenry to demonstrate against the desecration of Jewish graves. Feeding on that history, Ruchami tells Lippe: "Don't you dare come back here. Nazi."

When Lippe reports this call to Giti she is wearing a black dress decorated with red and green flowers. That poses her between her grief and her hope for renewal. After Ruchami threatens to expose

Lippe publicly, Giti and Lippe consider whether he should return. Alone, Giti presses the iron to her arm, against an emotional numbing. The rage Ruchami directs outward, Giti inflicts upon herself.

To protect her husband's secret, Giti travels to Rehevot for an unknown rabbi's counsel. He proposes a pragmatic course. If neither Giti or Ruchami has seen Lippe's gentile lover with their own eyes ("ocular proof")[9], it may not have happened. "People who are in crisis [as Lippe was] tend to imagine things.... We only relate to facts. Things we know for sure." So if they haven't actually seen Lippe's *shicksa* "the rest is — conjecture. We don't rely on conjecture." Given that "life flies by like a dream," perhaps we can convince ourselves that an unfortunate incident was but a dream. The argument confirms the drama's deliberate interweaving of disparate realities, from the very first scene on.

This is theological hairsplitting at its most constructive. It calls on faith in the face of evidence, but to a proper end: forgiveness in and for the family. However, this solution requires Giti to suppress what she does know and feel. This repression will prove another self-inflicted pain, like that iron, and a public humiliation.

And so Giti instructs Ruchami. As they lie in their beds, Giti lays out the new situation. She's having a wall built in the apartment so the girl can have her own bedroom. But Ruchami has to accept that everything she'd thought or been told about Lippe's misadventure was "a dream. None of it happened. He went away to work, he sent us money and will be coming home soon." This is a willful delusion.

Finally: "Don't you dare use my phone again without permission." Giti doesn't scold Ruchami or confront her threat. Instead, with the private room she offers security and respect for her daughter's maturing— then a stern correction. Nonetheless, she's imposing on Ruchami her own danger in denying a harsh truth.

Shulem's romantic aspirations have been dashed. Akiva edges toward an engagement. Giti's family balances on the precarious point of Lippe's return, Ruchami's rage and Giti's determination to deny a harsh reality. Elisheva closes the episode with advice more helpful

---

[9] From *Othello* where even this convincing proof can be deceptive.

than that rabbi's: "Turn the omelet over or it might burn." Loving is like that.

Episode I,11

The suppression theme continues in this episode — its motives and its dangers. The characters' attacks on Zionism make it the drama's most political episode.

A few minor suppressions play variations on that theme. Avoiding a complex discussion, Lippe answers yes when the younger son asks "Is it true only gentiles live abroad?" Lippe and Giti slip into Yiddish to discuss Ruchami's anger, over the other children's heads. These are harmless evasions.

More serious is the official suppression by which new principal Shulem asserts his authority. The children still think of their former teacher as their friend: "That's no way to run a school." He flexes his power by banning the "indecent custom" of watching the Independence Day air show: Zionist "airplanes celebrating the heresy of their leaders and their belief in the use of military might."

Here Shulem suppresses his real opinion. He earlier rejected Shoshanna's disdain for "the Zionist's celebration" of Israel's independence. As her husband contended, whoever watches the air shows and fireworks "is like someone who lights a cigarette off a burning Torah scroll.... It's forbidden to watch and that's all." Shulem disagreed: "It's only a bunch of planes making nice shapes in the sky." The *rebbetzin* tells Shulem to kiss her ass and walks away. "Such a mouth!" says Shulem. "Did she get it from her husband?"

Then— he cites her burning Torah image to support his ban at school. Compounding his hypocrisy of his ban, Shulem himself watches the air show from his office — smoking! More honest, Akiva allows his students to watch the airshow from the classroom, while he discreetly leaves (to phone Elisheva).

Their engagement party glosses several tensions. At the men's table the scribe pushes for an exact wedding date. Akiva stalls, sensing his need to consult with Elisheva who's with the women in the next room. The men decide. When Elisheva accepts Giti's congratulations she lightly cites their age gap: "Your little brother is a special man."

Ruchami has been suppressing the reality of *Anna Karenina* when reading it to her brothers at bedtime. She renamed the heroine Hannah, made her Jewish and bowdlerized her story. Yosa'le discovers the truth when he reads the hidden book to his brothers. "That's strange. Her name isn't Hannah. It's Anna. Must be a mistake." The intimacy disturbs them. "Why does she let him kiss her hand?" "I don't know. I must have taken the wrong book." The suppressed will eventually emerge, with a vengeance.

Having read to the end, Yosa'le confronts Ruchami with her deception. "How could you do that? How could you tell us that story?" His response is harshly unforgiving: "You're a liar…. I never want to talk to you again…. I don't believe you anymore." Ruchami admits her sin and promises never to lie to Yosa'le again.

Immediately she lies— to hide her aborted plan to post their father's shame. This justifiable falseness, like her faking her father's letters, are constructive pretences to conceal Lippe's betrayal.

The episode's three most dramatic scenes expose the danger of such suppression, whether of the truth or of emotions:

(i) Akiva and Elisheva have observed all appropriate decorum in their courtship. Now officially engaged, he brings her to his studio to paint her. When she sees a reproduction of a Chagall white-gowned bride she pauses her pose to go out. She replaces her plain black dress with the white gown a Russian seamstress made for her first wedding.

In her absence Akiva has dozed off. He dreams of his mother in the kitchen, crying over chopped carrots: "In heaven everything makes you cry." It's a heavenly freedom to express emotions suppressed on earth. She cries from concern over Akiva and Elisheva. "But what can I do? I love her."

After the dream Akiva is further unsettled by Elisheva's breathtaking beauty and by her sensuality, sniffing his scarf. He can't paint her; he'll resume tomorrow. When Elisheva comes kiss-close he retreats. "Not now. Tomorrow. Okay?" That's for the painting. A kiss must await the wedding.

On the phone, struggling against the Independence Day planes' roar above, Akiva tells Elisheva he can't stand their long engagement. He wants to marry and to live with her, to complete their relationship.

(ii) Giti struggles to suppress Lippe's betrayal. She greets his return with a beaming smile but they don't touch. At night they repair to their separate beds. When she summons him back in to Akiva's engagement party he feels alienated: "Everyone's so nice to me. Thanks for not telling anyone." "There was nothing to tell," she insists. "Nothing happened, understand? Nothing happened."

Her denial of reality proves selfish. It denies Lippe his need to confess, to apologize, to repent. Refusing "to talk about it," she cites the rabbi: "Maybe you had a strange dream."

Giti's suppression ends in a public eruption in a store, *The World of Fashion* (the world as distinct from her community). Acting out her cheery confidence, she dons a bright dress, white at the top with lower layers in Israeli-flag blue. The brightness and — in context — faint Zionism are a false front.

Giti's mirror reflection is violated by a brassy woman in a short skirt and high heels, chattering on her cell phone. Her image thus displaced and her guard down, Giti assaults her, screaming "*Shicksa. Swine. Get the *shicksa* out of here."* This fatuous innocent has become the enemy *shicksa* Giti struggled to deny. After, Giti crouches in the alley, sobbing, humiliated beyond what Lippe did to her.

(iii) In contrast to Giti's denial, Ruchami confronts Lippe's betrayal. She proceeds with her threat to expose him with 100 posters, which above his photograph blare "Lippe Weiss / A Criminal / Left his family." When the tape she uses at night doesn't hold, she arises early, mixes up paste and goes to post them.

But then Yosa'le confronts her with her lies about her bedtime story. As she admits her own guilt, she loses her righteous fervour. She drops her plan. When Lippe enters, Ruchami throws the posters at him. To prevent her brothers' shame, she's not posting them. Shame had not deterred her before. Shame at having lied to her brothers does now.

Ruchami's open anger allows Lippe the honesty Giti denied him. As he stoops to clean up the mess, he opens out to his daughter: "You're right. I am evil and I know I'm going to hell. But neither you nor your brothers nor your righteous mother deserve to be without a father. That's the only reason I decided to come back."

He also strikes a note to which she can relate. Married at 19, he found himself with a wife, family, responsibilities, "the frenzy to make money— to care, to listen, to embrace, to love." He yearned to walk down the street not caring about anyone or having anyone care about him. Hence his inexcusable impulse to flee. For a girl just given her own bedroom, this loss of freedom registers.

How does she signal some acceptance of her father? By giving him womanly advice: "You have to sweep up the flour with a broom."

Ruchami gave him what Giti denied him: the chance to confront what he did, to end the suppression. "Thank you for listening to me, Ruchami. I needed that. Good night."

During the Independence Day air show Ruchami sits on her bed, shredding the posters that would have been a disastrous assertion of her own independence. She flings a confetti pile of them out the window. *Rebbitzin* Erblich spits and walks away, eyes downward.

Like Giti's self-abasing campaign to protect her husband's reputation — and in the next episode, her decision on an abortion — Ruchami's decision not to shame Lippe places the family good ahead of her personal will. This flies in the face of our mainstream liberal spirit. In both cases the women find fulfilment — even perhaps an alternative independence? — within the strictures of their society, not in escaping them. While exposing the callous patriarchy, *Shtisel* also poses a serious challenge to the Western religion, absolute individualism.

Episode I, 12

The season closes on his children's hopes dashed by Shulem's selfish insularity, his fear of impurity. Here he causes at least two miseries. They are rooted in the question Zvi Arye poses Lippe in the yeshiva: "Is it prohibited because the law applies to a person or to an object?" People have rights, needs and wills that objects don't. Disregarding one's humanity leads to all this episode's suffering.

In the opening scene Akiva declines, then at least delays, Elisheva's invitation to move to London. "It's so different than here," she says, which attracts her but frightens him. She would work; he could paint. "Will you marry me in London? "I don't know. But we'll be able to take our time." Elisheva could ease Akiva into a freer relationship outside their community's restrictions.

When Fuchs sees Akiva's loving painting of Elisheva he claims the right to sign and exhibit it as his work in *Earthy Jerusalem*, a group show at the Jewish Museum. "They want an Orthodox artist." Fuchs imposes an allegorical reading upon Akiva's portrait of Elisheva. In II,12 Shulem disastrously imposes his wife's identity on Akiva's allegorical painting. Yet another example of this drama's elegantly detailed construction.

Unlike his earlier surrender of his grandparents' portrait, Akiva now denies Fuchs, physically fighting to keep the work. As in the yeshiva question Fuchs claims the object because he provided the studio and the materials of its creation. Akiva's claim lies in humanity — his commitment to its subject. Fuchs expels him from his studio.

Shulem arrogates the responsibility to eliminate impurity. When Zvi Arye's son Velvale is tossed from choir for swearing, Shulem makes it a personal mission. He assigns the lad lines, then accuses Malka of exposing his grandson to the vulgarities of TV. The *rebbetzin* is less pure: "What did he say? *Schmuck*?... What did he say? Butt? *Putz*? What?"

At her Bingo game, with stern words and harsh looks Shulem cows his sad mother into guilt. That night her dream of herself and her husband at dinner is overrun by the soundtrack of a TV drama. She awakens in a panic and phones Shulem to remove the set immediately. "You were right. You saved me." Television is "the angel of death incarnate." Akiva obliges, but only after his grandmother assures him she does want the TV gone.

Malka regrets this sacrifice immediately. Her Psalms are not as engaging. A small pale ceramic is no substitute for the TV's human interest. What happened to Ridge? She begs to watch Shoshanna's set but she only watches the news. "Go to the lobby and watch with that *schmuck* Zilberman who changes channels every minute."

So — because Shulem feared the impurities of TV he deprived his mother of its pleasure, dooming her to the lobby set, *en route* to which she falls down the stairs and into a coma. An unintended consequence is still a consequence.

Shulem similarly "rescues" Akiva from his misery. Shulem considers the twice-widow impure, inappropriate for his son. Now Akiva disastrously seeks his advice about Elisheva's reluctance to remarry. Shulem recalls an aunt, Malka's sister, whose playmate fell into a well and drowned. Chaya ("animal") bore an irrational guilt for that death for years, finally jumping to her death at 30. "Why did you tell me that?" Akiva asks. "No reason. It just came to mind." But Malka never heard of that sister. Shulem invented that character and story to support his position. His family "history" is a lie.

Shulem holds Elisheva responsible for her husbands' deaths. He ambushes her at home, urging her to get out of Akiva's life altogether. "If you really cared for him you wouldn't make his life so miserable." He says Akiva agrees that she can't marry him because she can't forgive herself "for what you did to your husbands." This, of course, is nonsense, as we see from her scenes with them. Shulem lies to Akiva, then about him, to end his son's romance.

Obeying, Elisheva phones Akiva from the airport: "Get back to your life before you met me, before I got in your way.... I know that this is what you want." "No, it isn't." "Then why did you tell him?" His love now lost, Akiva confronts his father: "You talked to her, didn't you?... I want nothing to do with you."

In despair, Akiva sells his treasured painting of Elisheva to the shady Fuchs and lets him sign it. Invited back into the fold — "You see? We found a compromise" —Akiva leaves: "I'm never touching a paintbrush again."

Like that of TV, Giti fears the "filth" Lippe brings home on his cellphone internet: "Why should a yeshiva student need the internet?" Lippe makes cartoons instead of considering the yeshiva points of debate: "The Babylonian and Jerusalem *Talmuds* differ on the laws of dry figs and raisins that were dried on a roof." Even fruitful Bible study can be arid.

Lippe would rather be a businessman, like Glicksberg, the lucky (*glick*) success who supports many dedicated students. Lippe buys a cell phone (on five instalments) to prepare for a possible job as Glicksberg's (unpaid) errand boy, hoping to work up to a salary. That's another form of faith slightly better than Sucher's lottery ticket.

Lippe loses even this faint opening when Giti takes a six-day women's retreat. He feels victim. "How can you do this to me, Giti?... How can I stay alone with the kids? I've never been alone with them for more than a few hours." "Ruchami will help. She's used to that." Giti throws up his past: "I'll be back. You know that. But every time you leave the house I have to wonder if you'll come back."

48

Lippe lacks parental patience. He breaks the younger son's hopeful "candy tree." This recalls Shulem's rejecting his children's aspirations as "fantasies." "You want candy, get a job and buy some," insists the jobless father, truant from his paid studies.

Giti's "retreat" proves a euphemism. She registers at a hotel, the Palatin, so cheap it hasn't replaced the missing O in H-tel. Her motive becomes clear when she faces an interview — for an abortion.

The presiding male — of course — Dr Sagi seems kind, offering kosher mints, but he proceeds to a bullying cross-examination to discourage the woman's initiative. This is the patriarchy in full weed. Against his "unethical" pressure, Giti is firm: "I can barely keep my life together as it is." The woman on the committee assures Giti: "The decision to abort a pregnancy is yours and yours alone." Giti wears the prison-stripe top she wore when she consulted the distant rabbi about Lippe's return (I,10).

Giti nervously signs the two required forms. But when the nurse leaves to determine the operating room, Lippe phones to report Malka's coma. Whether or not Giti takes this as a sign from God, she tears up the forms and rushes to the hospital.

When she throws herself, weeping, on her grandmother it is her brother Zvi Arye not her father who rises to comfort her. Whichever one's perspective, Giti's avoidance of either (i) having a sixth child with an unreliable husband or (ii) having an abortion, is another consequence of Shulem's attack on the impurity of his mother's TV.

Note that we have not seen any physical contact or emotional reconnection between Giti and Lippe. Even his departure in I,1 was chilled. Upon his return the conventional film would have given us at least an embrace, with a discreet cutaway to a fireplace, a fountain, fireworks, perhaps a subtle train entering a tunnel. Here, nothing. This authorial choice is a matter of moral as well as aesthetic reticence. This drama respects sexuality— as its subject community does — by according it total privacy.

The dawn brings new hope. Ruchami repaired and furnished Benyamin's "candy tree." The boy is ecstatic, his capacity to hope restored: "I'll share with everyone. You too, Father." That's the father who destroyed his fantasy. Giti tells Lippe she's having another baby.

This hopefulness, this faith in humanity in the face of loss, reappears when Shulem dumps his sermon for the school's prayer book event. With his mother unconscious in the hospital, he realized not a word of it was true.

Instead he admits that all the times his mother cried over lighting the *shabbes* candles, she was crying on demand, at the prayer book's injunction. Shulem found her real emotional life in the paper that fell out of her prayer book: a list of names, all her grandchildren, her great-grandchildren — and some names he didn't recognize. Ridge, son of Stephanie. Brook, daughter of Cynthia. Characters in her favourite TV drama.

The properly segregated school audience is appalled that their principal let his mother watch TV. Faculty members mitigate Shulem's humiliation: he's tired, he should step down, don't disgrace yourself further.

This ritual event is shattered by Shulem's rare respect for emotion. This is a remarkable breakthrough for him, out from formality into genuine feeling: "My esteemed teachers, here I must cry: How powerful is your love, Mother, love even for people who don't exist in reality." This is Shulem's most human, most compassionate, scene in the entire first season.

But he retreats to rote formula in his closing blessing upon the kids: "I hope that your hearts will always be pure. That you will always care for each other. That you will always pray."

Despite this brief evidence of human warmth and humility, the damage Shulem has done is done. As Akiva watches his Elisheva hanged in the gallery he loses his love, his vocation, his sense of self. In Malka's room he and Shulem exchange silent glances.

Then something astonishing occurs — an unprecedented moment of meta-cinema. The camera draws back to reveal that the supposed life scene is actually appearing on a TV screen — watched from heaven by the white garbed spirits of Malka and her husband Velvale. This link between life on earth and in the heavens is the culmination of the season's interweaving of different levels of reality (dream, memory, the return of the dead, and the character's "life" which is itself a fiction — as ours is, in the context of spirituality, an illusion). As Malka enjoys in heaven the medium that her son forbade on earth, we are again reminded of the arbitrariness of man's rules, conventions and prohibitions, which from another perspective dwindle into nothing.

The season that began with Akiva's dream of his dead mother ends with the fantasy of his dying grandmother. The celestial television scene ending Season One echoes the ending of the first episode, when Malka was left with her set disconnected, reduced to watching snow. Here she can watch her real life with the interest she'd enjoyed on TV, but beside her dearly departed husband.

"Are you going back," her Velvale asks her, in heaven, "or staying?"

For which do we hope?

* * *

The actress who played Malka, Hanna Rieber, died in Tel Aviv on September 9, 2014, at 87. So, the actress "stayed" up there. But the character returned for Season Two, via Leah Koenig. The creators divided actor and role, rather than allow the character to die with her actor. The character had a further role to perform.

Here is the human predicament. We want to be angels but are tempted to such sins as selfishness, righteousness, vanity. The menu extends. We learn our moral lessons, but they may not cover the complexities of real life. Especially on matters of the heart. Even what we forbid — *e.g.*, a choice in love, an influence like television— or what we value and propound — *e.g.*, fealty to a superior authority, to a traditional institution or to an absolute value, whether religious orthodoxy or Western liberalism — may not prove sufficient when considered from an alternative perspective. Hence this drama's promotion of compassion over rules — but also its respect for the communal construct that may prove a salutary alternative to the untrammelled individual will.

Season Two

Episode II,1

Like the first season's opener, II,1 starts with a dream (here Shulem's) and closes on a memory (Akiva's). The show continues to interweave our different levels of consciousness.

Shulem's dream grows out of the heavenly fantasy that closed Season One. He drives a supposedly conscious Malka to visit her husband Velvale's grave. She finds the cemetery organization beautiful. When Shulem is locked out of the car, it rolls away from him. "You forgot your walker," he calls pointlessly. "You use it," she says, "I'm moving on" — an echo of Shulem's parting from Edna. Then Malka adds intriguing advice: "Take care of that belly button, my child." Shulem awakens to patting his stomach.

The line is a reminder of Shulem's physical vulnerability, especially as regards the umbilicus, the two-way connection between parent and child. As it happens, "belly button" is one of the funnier words in Yiddish: *pupick*.[10] But the reference here is serious indeed. In Shulem's subconscious his mother is reminding him of the quintessential human link, the bond of birth and the mutual responsibilities between parent and child. This is another passing detail on which the whole drama can be taken to pivot.

Shulem awakens to find his mother still in her coma. His brother Nachum has arrived from Belgium, but he wants to eat and sleep before seeing her. Shulem condemns this lack of filial care, but the brothers are equally selfish.

Worse, Nachum's next-day visit snaps Malka out of her eight-month coma! When Shulem arrives, she doesn't recognize him. Nachum was always her favourite. As Shulem notes, "The youngest is always the youngest" (He forgets his dashed hope for Adi in I,10).

Out of her coma, Malka thinks Ruchami is her own sister Pessia. Back at the seniors' residence, Malka keeps calling Shoshanna "Freide," despite correction and her usual "Kiss my ass." More confusion: Tenenbaum stole Zukerman's teeth to avenge theft of his pants.

---

[10] Martin Scorsese flirts with it in naming the antihero of *King of Comedy* Rupert Pupkin.

That absurdity sets up Malka's new romance. She discovers her lost Velvale in an ex-grocer named Maurice Badihi. They regale each other with smatters of memory, even though they speak different languages, she Yiddish and he Arabic. Shoshanna tells Shulem Malka spent the night with him: "If you don't want any more siblings get here right away."

To thwart that romance Shulem takes Malka to the cemetery. He shows her their spouses' graves and her reserved site. He repeats that he's her son; he has cared for her all his life. Then Shulem turns cruel: her favoured Nachum "doesn't care about you at all." In his 15 years in Belgium "he came to see you just once —and that was to take away your apartment." Malka snaps back into awareness — and tears.

Nachum is a colourful character. A fast-talking hustler, he exercises the traditional comic stereotype of the Jew. He's brusque with the nurses, indeed with everybody. "I hate hospitals in this country....You know how much Zionists pay them for a bed? They should be ashamed." He damns the luggage handlers.

Nachum and Libbi move into Shulem's, uninvited. Sbulem finds them finishing his food in the kitchen. "Make yourself at home," Nachum greets him. Nachum intends to claim Malka's apartment, so Libbi can marry a Torah scholar. Against this claim Shulem's only argument is that Malka has let Zvi Arye live there free for many years so that should continue. Shulem offers to help Nachum finance an apartment for Libbi. What Shulem strikingly does *not* say here is his earlier claim that he is paying the mortgage on this property, among his claimed six (one per child). Another Shulem lie is exposed.

Over this Nachum and Shulem refuse to speak to each other. Instead they send messages through Libbi and Akiva, though all four are together. The brothers' refusal to communicate contrasts to the cheery harmony that Malka and Maurice (her "Velvale") achieve despite not understanding each other's language. Which pair are sane?

As Libbi and Akiva bridge their fathers' alienation, the episode develops the cousins' romantic possibility. They exchange interested glances and smiles. Akiva casually asks Libbi's age. When Nachum urges Akiva to find a wife he's already barring him from Libbi. Prophetically, Akiva says "I hope Libbi is comfortable in my bed" (He has given her his room). Typifying the culture's sexual sensitivity,

Shulem insists on switching beds with Akiva, because a son shouldn't sleep in his mother's bed, even alone.

When the cousins flee their snoring fathers, they meet in their pyjamas on the balcony. The Piamenta Brothers that Libbi cites are a popular Chabad musical duo that were discovered by jazz musician Stan Getz. The allusion cites the Shtisel brothers' nasal airs. Libbi hasn't heard of Akiva's two failed engagements. Nachum has brought her along determined to find her a marriage.

In the chill Akiva drapes his blanket over her and recalls a treasured childhood incident. As children they were on that balcony the day before Nachum moved the family to Belgium. Akiva suggested a contest: Each had to eat a sour lemon without grimacing. As she was leaving, Libbi bent over and kissed him on the cheek. Now she has no memory of that incident. The episode ends with Akiva remembering his younger self's smile at that kiss.

In a variation on the "look after your *pupick*" theme, *i.e.*, the continuing maternal connection, Lippe and Giti interview for the chance to earn $50,000 by naming their coming son Zelig, to honour a childless man who would otherwise have no-one to say *kaddish* (the prayer for the dead) in his name. The Weisses find a roomful of orthodox couples "all praying to be Zelig's parents," monetizing the *pupick*.

In their interview Renta Beyfus[11] senses that Giti doesn't share Lippe's enthusiasm for the deal ($25,000 on signing the contract, $25,000 after the naming). As Renta's mother was also named Giti they have a potential bond. But Giti is reserved: "I feel strange selling ... my baby's name. This is my child. Flesh of my flesh. How would you feel...." Renta can't identify with motherhood, so she asks for the next applicant: "To each what God gave them."

Thus reminded of the divine miracle of birth, Giti responds with a generous offer. They will oblige her but with no compensation: "We'll name him Zelig for the love of God. To elevate your husband's name." By this integrity Giti wins the contract. Lippe's "divine providence" hinges on Giti's rejection of his "honest pay." Of course, he sneaks back to tell Renta that he and Giti are willing to accept a small payment — if only to make Renta "feel better." He gets a fat envelope.

---

[11] Another telling name: "Renta" as in rent-a-womb?

Why "Zelig"? The name — "blessed" —is ironic for a success-ful man *not* blessed with a child. Woody Allen's brilliant 1964 film of that name created a new connotation: a character of shifting identities, like a chameleon, but lacking a moral core.[12] As he'll be Lippe's son, both meanings pertain.

While Lippe monetizes his next child, Ruchami plans to marry an ultra-religious student. Stopping to tie a loose shoelace, she over-hears a young man's praying to be "saved from doubts… and impure thoughts. Forbidden sights and nocturnal emission." He prays to be "totally immersed in the Torah. I can't take these thoughts, dear God. I only want to be immersed in You. Day and night, Father, day and night." Ruchami sets out to wed him, despite her community's conven-tions of courtship. She is the answer to his prayers.

The boy isn't there when Ruchami returns in makeup. The next time she proposes: "I can save you, I can help you live a pure life…. You'll focus on your studies, day and night." He flees.

The 15-year-old Ruchami is precocious in this campaign. But we have watched her prepare, as she cared for her siblings, especially when Giti had to work. Her idealism allows her aggressiveness. The match seems destined beyond their religious conventions. For this fer-vidly religious and constant boy is also the answer to Ruchami's unar-ticulated prayers — the antithesis to her father.

Her religious motive is supported by the need for independence that she picked up from *Middlemarch* and *Anna Karenina*. Both ro-mances center on passionate heroines, the spiritual Dorothea and the romantic Anna. In her young scholar Ruchami finds a combination of George Eliot's old, arid pedant Casaubon and the more devoted young Ladislaw. Indeed the homonymy of her *Hannah* Karenina and this *Hanina* suggests her romantic dream has taken human form.

Unlike those heroines, however, Ruchami satisfies her rebel-lion within the strictures of her community and faith, not against or outside it. That is a credit both to the rewards of that faith and to this believer's self-knowledge.

---

[12] When the *Oxford English Dictionary* website made 'zelig' its word of the day it defined it by the Woody Allen usage.

Episode II, 2

The two main plot-lines interweave two themes: betrayals and beginnings.

The major betrayal is Lippe's proceeding — against Giti's ardent wishes — to name their son Zelig. When Ruchami needs Lippe to call a cab for Giti's delivery, he is away investing the Beyfus payment with a broker. As "The stock market is like legal Russian Roulette," Shtruck recommends foreign currency. Lippe wants a safe investment, for his children's sake as well as for his own ego. "Keep in touch," Shtruck says in English, as Giti's nurse will say "Okay"— as if English is extra assuring. Unwittingly Lippe investing in foreign currency amplifies Giti's venture into currency exchange.

Gitti needs Lippe to attend her delivery, which Jewish law forbids. So he sings on his cell phone from the balcony, where he's smoking. As he sings her request, *Contentment and Gladness, Light for the Jews*, their new son emerges on the line "God is the rock of the universe." Lippe also steadies the interloping Renta: "Giti never screams when she's having a baby."

Giti was disturbed by Renta's visit, even when she brings in the head of the obstetrics ward: "What I really need is to be left alone." Worse, she awakens to an empty crib. Renta took the baby out, claiming to be Giti's mother. "You were sleeping so soundly. I'm sorry." Renta knows she went too far.

Fearing Renta's interference, Giti would rescind their naming agreement. Lippe doesn't admit he has taken — and invested — her fee. That's how he could book her into a recuperation center for new mothers. He deflects: "I feel bad. We promised." "Why deny her that grace?" Finally, "You rest. I'll talk to her…. I'll make up some excuse. Some grandfather we forgot about."

To his credit, Lippe tries to withdraw the money but Shtruck won't let him. He graphs their projected income: "You and your wife will thank me for this" — despite its threat to their "marital peace." In this, the man's world — "Who tells his wife about business?" — the woman's will and needs are disregarded. No respect for the *pupick*.

At the naming ceremony Lippe prays with intensity, though nervous about Giti's presence upstairs. The rabbi has to ask the baby's name twice, as if Lippe still hasn't decided. He whispers it to him. As

Ruchami notes, hearing her son named Zelig erases Giti's smile. She looks down on her misnamed son, the helpless center of that all-male world from which she, her will and her gender are excluded. Lippe is roundly congratulated — having again broken his wife's trust

In addition to Zelig's beginning, the episode advances Ruchami's own romance. As she feeds her brothers, she rubs her own tummy when a brother asks: "All the people in the world come out of their mummies' bellies, right?""*Rechem*" or "womb" lurks in the name "Ruchami." To emphasize her maturing, in the opening scene Ruchami jokes to Giti that their class was just lectured on clothing choice. When Giti brings Zelig home Lippe asks Ruchami to make dinner but she stands up to him: "You make the salad. I'll make the omelet." She's suspicious about her mother's troubled reaction to the naming.

In the episode's second betrayal Shulem undermines Akiva's interest in art. When Libbi is impressed by her cousin's drawings, he offers them to her: "I'm not into it anymore." Her response encourages him: "If God had given me such a gift, such a talent, I'd do my best not to waste it." That advances their kinship and Akiva's art career.

Her encouragement prompts Akiva to take a morning off work to show his work to some galleries. When he comes into Libbi's room to collect his drawings she asks "Where are you taking them?" His reply hows a new seriousness about his work: "I don't know. I'll see where they take me."

They take him against his father. Shulem refuses his request for time off. "I thought you were done with these fantasies" — Shulem's usual term for his children's ambitions. As for that "gift from God, no less. Maybe it came with a gift receipt?" This division will intensify at the end of Season Two. To Shulem, art and religion are antithetical. For Akiva, art is a spiritual practice akin to religion.

Hearing that Akiva asked Aliza to find him a sub, Shulem orders her to send the class home and to tell Akiva he's fired. That is the "worst that could happen," as Akiva asked rhetorically, preparing to show his work to dealer Izzie Kaufman.

The firing frees Akiva to go with Libbi to shop in Tel Aviv. Both react nervously when a passenger gives up his seat so Libbi can join her "husband." They appear *bashert* — destined to unite. When Libbi dozes off, her head on Akiva's shoulder, he settles into that impropriety. "I'm with a girlfriend," she tells Nachum, when he calls her back to meet her first prospect: "not a nerd….the *creme de la creme*."

When Akiva and Libbi return, Shulem is suspicious: "You were out together?" He avoids his fired son's look. Akiva wishes Libbi luck with his rival. At Nachum's request, he gets pop and a poppy cake for her "date," then sets it out for them and discreetly departs.

To recover his job Shulem requires Akiva write an official handwritten apology and pledge never to repeat his sin again. "Like you're writing to your boss…. It's not for me but for you. That way maybe you'll stop roaming around like a runny-nosed little boy in the *shtetl*." The demand is humiliating.

Akiva writes that letter and leaves it beside his father, who (as usual) fell asleep at the table reading. Akiva draws him. That powerful force looks so weak here, unguarded, sprawled on the table, his *yarmulke* off, fingers reaching out to nothing. Strengthened by his art, Akiva junks his apology.

When Kaufman first saw Akiva's drawings he found mere talent: "They're pleasant at best…. Fluff." Had Akiva valued one work he would have brought it alone. At the new drawing of Shulem, Kaufman asks Akjiva his name again: "Shtisel, this will do. Nice to meet you, Shtisel." Akiva makes his name as an artist, just as baby Zelig receives his troubled name. Both beginnings survive their betrayals.

Meanwhile, the brothers' egos threaten their children's unity. When Shulem asks if the couch is comfortable Nachum bristles: "Don't worry. I won't inconvenience you forever." Shulem continues to lie: he tells Konigsberg the 23-year-old Libbi is 21. Compulsively insulting, Nachum wants "a studious, earnest young man, not a loser in orthopedic shoes." And yet…. Nachum's recognition of a Tchaikovsky on the radio foreshadows the revelation of his lost ardor for classical music. Amid all these betrayals, every beginning carries new hope.

Episode II,3

The two framing shots make Giti the episode's central character. It opens on her, depressed, in the new mothers' retreat. She's unresponsive to Zelig's crying until roommate Mina rouses her and suggests she seek counseling. In the closing shot Giti beams happily after singing to her family — *sans* Lippe — at Shulem's.

Giti's *post-partum* fatigue is compounded by grief that Lippe sold their son's name against her will. At home, Ruchami pushes Lippe to explain: "She was never like this before." Lippe's "Nothing happened" is Giti's strategy of strained denial.

A charity fund-raiser drops by with a talking parrot, which Lippe buys to cheer up Giti. When that doesn't work he asks "Are you trying to get back at me for thinking of our future? Our children's future?" — as if she chooses to be depressed. Here Giti again wears a prison-stripe dress, but warmer, inflected pink. She responds to Shulem's funny faces, how he cheered *post-partum* Dvora. Shulem is for once charming and considerate.

The parrot is a significant symbol. It has been trained to repeat what it hears, including the admonition "No bad words for a righteous parrot." But when it tries to say "Lippe" it comes out "Klippah." The word denotes an unholy shell that prevents goodness both from entering the holiness within and from seeing reality.[13] Given Lippe's generosity, though, his essential goodness is belied by the hard shell of his abetting Giti's later assault on Ruchami's marriage. The bird's mistake tells a larger truth. There's also a comic effect in the incongruity between its feathered animal nature and its human speech.[14]

Of course, sounding human does not make one human, especially if one is a bird. Correspondingly, the appearance of compassion may not prove humanity even in humans. As a parrot can sound human without being human, so can people. We have seen Lippe inhumanely betray Giti twice. Whatever his motives, words or even consequence, his betrayal is a betrayal. Nachum and Shulem impede their children's happiness despite their ostensible care. Both fathers fail their loved ones even as they may parrot caring for them.

Unable to manage the home, especially in Ruchami's absence, Lippe makes a dramatic move. He sends all the young children in a taxi to Giti's retreat: "Dad said we should ask if you remember us." Ruchami is outraged that Lippe endangered his children, Giti that he would deploy them against her. She takes them home — to Shulem's.

---

13 For this insight I'm grateful to Yerachmiel Chaim Beiles.

14 Henri Bergson's *Theory of Comedy* roots the genre in just such incongruity.

In that reunion Akiva's blessing over his (plain) pizza rings resonant: "Blessed are You, Lord, who creates various kinds of sustenance." Those sustenances go beyond the pizza and cola. They include the warmth of the family, the harmony of the music, how Giti recovers her spirit by playing the accordion, and how Ruchami acts on her impulse to leave her yeshiva beau food. He responds. Giti's song plays across all these scenes — plus Lippe sleeping on his couch, at home, with his silly parrot but outside his family.

Though the episode focuses on the Weisses' dysfunction it's balanced by framing scenes of Akiva and Libbi at play. In the first, on the balcony they riff satirically on what the elderly couple below might be saying — largely fuss and fear. The Shtisel balcony is often an escape from the restrictions inside the flat, an opening onto the outside world, however restrictive that neighbourhood.

By playing an old couple Akiva and Libbi are testing couplehood. Libbi reports that her Cohen date "was nice and they say he's very serious….. Don't worry, Akiva, no-one says that about you." But Libbi considers herself very serious. When Akiva ventures a romantic opening, Libbi deflects it.

Shulem scolds Akiva for "sitting with a woman so frivolously." For the cousins are no longer children. Sensing their attraction, Shulem broaches to Nachum the idea of cousins marrying. Their grandparents were cousins. It used to be quite common. Nachum responds in distaste: "Back then people ate chicken feet too." "I still buy chicken feet," admits Shulem, "They're tasty and cheap."[15] When Shulem again suggests matching their two "slightly screwed up" kids, Nachum won't accept the "third rate bum" Akiva for his "princess."

Akiva returns to the brothers' frigid silence. Libbi and Nachum are moving out, to Shulem's relief. "If you want to get married," Shulem advises, "you'll have to do something about your snoring." This is classic projection. Akiva is neither the snorer that Shulem is nor the *schnorrer* (con) that Nachum is.

If only to oppose Nachum, Shulem helps Akiva. He bribes Farshlufen to call Nachum and pretend to arrange a second meeting for Libby and Cohen. Shulem rouses Akiva to send him to a new match-

---

[15] I'm with Shulem on this one.

maker's setup. And so Akiva and Libby connect at 7:30, their fake 7 pm dates having disappointed them. "We've both been stood up," says Akiva, so why not have their own "match meeting."

After playing an elderly couple, they play at being themselves on an introductory date. In the usual small talk, Akiva has found that it's "a three-cigarette walk" from home to this lobby. His order — "two bitter lemons with ice" — recalls their childhood contest with lemons when, he remembers fondly, she kissed his cheek. "Nobody told me you have green eyes," Libbi says. "Nobody told me you are so pretty," he replies.

As Ruchami pursues her romance, she sees her scholar dozing over a book, unable to memorize the injunction against leavened bread. To rise himself, he eats two spoons of instant coffee. On her next visit she leaves him food with a note: "Healthy food will help you study better." He replies: "Thank God. It did help me study better." Thanking God is his way to thank her.

The Cohens' mysterious silence is due to match-maker Konigsberg's sudden death, when he fell off his ladder. His myriad customers are lost: "How can we go on?" Indeed, assistant Farshlufen hasn't "been able to sleep ever since."

In the match-maker's coded notebook Nachum makes out Konigsberg's summary of Shulem: "Smokes and eats." Indignant, Shulem tears out the incriminating page: "Blessed is the *true* judge."

Shulem is so insulted by that reduction he declines Aliza's offer of her lunch. Earlier, when she failed to offer him a taste he instructed her henceforth to eat in the staff room, at regular times, not in the office: "It's for your benefit." Now, when Shulem asks how she would describe him she redeems herself: "Father and educator." His vanity appeased, Shulem can (i) again share Aliza's lunch, and (ii) tell Akiva to put just that phrase on his tombstone. Shulem validates Konigsberg's reduction. Aliza handles him through his eating and his fuming.

Episode II, 4

At the one-third season mark this episode introduces an unaccustomed violence. The episode is framed by Holocaust references, moving from war to peace.

In the opening scene the boys at Anshin's play a violent video game, killing evil "Germans" — though the villains are black. If we're relieved that the opening gunshots are in a game, the relief is temporary. In the last scene, as Shoshanna drifts into her fatal overdose, her TV announces a new documentary: "Germany: 70 years later." Young Germans come to Israel to meet Holocaust survivors. Death and rebirth come together.

Both violent video game scenes end in romantic possibilities. In the first, suitor Yakov Cohen seeks out Akiva to convey his marital interest in Libbi. In the second, Ruchami interrupts the game so the men will witness her formal declaration of marriage to Hanina Tonik. In contrast to the Gottlieb wedding plan, this table is simply set with beer, cigarettes and torn challah. (The Haredi marriage requires only the oath and three witnesses. Indeed the community outside the film debated whether this ceremony formally married the two actors!)

Irritated by his grandchildren's noise, Shulem counsels Giti, under the guise of selflessness, to go home. As he says Dvora used to tell him, "Let me help you carry the weight." Giti clears Lippe of suspicion of violence toward her. She just needs time to work out her feelings. Shulem hopes she's not blinded by anger: "The children come first. Ruchami is almost 16. How can she find a marriage if you get a divorce?" Overhearing that hardens Ruchami's resolve to marry, if only to free Giti from Lippe. She proceeds to the Vilna Synagogue where she enters the room, introduces herself to the frightened Hanina, and joins him in warm smiles.

Now the game's violence spreads into life. When Ruchami introduces her husband, Lippe floors him with a punch. He responded to Hanina saying he has "consecrated" his bride, a term Lippe may have found ambiguous.[16] Ruchami leaves coldly: "If you want to apologize and say congratulations, we'll be at the Vilna synagogue."

After his violence, Lippe grows sympathetic to Hanina. He assures Giti the boy is not "a rebel" but a nice person. He was carrying a *Talmud*! As the boys at Anshin's discover, Hanina is unknown, descending from neither the sardine nor the *Chevra Kadisha* (funeral so-

---

[16] Elena Geron points out that the Hebrew phrase is "Behold, you are consecrated to me." It gained in the translation.

ciety) Toniks. (In II,3 the Shtisel brothers determine that Libbi's suitor is from neither the candy nor the candle Cohens.) The unknown boy takes on the others' projections, whether hopes or fears. "Hanina" connotes graciousness and mercy, the qualities he provides to and draws from Ruchami.

Giti approves Lippe's violence: "You should have hit [the scoundrel] harder." Dismissing the marriage as one of Ruchami's "dreams" echoes the "fantasies" that Shulem declares his children's ambitions. Going to retrieve Ruchami, Lippe picks up a wooden staff. At the window he sees the couple talking happily over beers. Lippe drops the weapon and leaves. Accepting his daughter's marriage, Lippe begins to redeem himself for his earlier failure.

The only violence in Akiva's courtship of Libbi is Nachum's opposition. Akiva pays the seniors' home clerk to phone when Libbi visits Malka, so Akiva can "coincidentally" appear. He explains he brought Cohen to Nachum because "I wanted to talk to you." About what? "Whatever." At the art exhibition Akiva jokes that if Libbi steps over the viewer's line three times the security guard will shoot her. "What would I do without you?" "What would you?" The cousins approach their feelings, then retreat.

Akiva wants her to see two paintings by Mauricio Gottlieb. One is the artist's anguished self-portrait, the other of his beautiful fiancee. He died at 23, before they could marry. Ironically, the artist combines the names of Malka's senile beau and Akiva's ex-fiancee. But he is an actual Polish painter (1856-1879). Life is art.

This art frees Akiva to speak: "I don't want to die that way. I want to live a normal life," with a wife and family. When he asks Libbi to skip her Cohen date she flees: "That's okay…. I have to go." Their conversations are painful balances between their desire to connect and their inculcated inhibitions.

One tune plays over Akiva lying on his balcony, smoking sadly, and Libbi listening to her date's chat, obviously distracted. The bridging song suggests the separated cousins' connection.

Nachum has rejected Akiva. When Akiva brings rival Cohen to the hotel, Nachum sends his regards to Shulem. But when Akiva sends regards to Libbi Nachum rescinds his own civility: "You know what? Don't say anything." Now he pushes her to marry Cohen. He drinks the glass of water he says she needs. Like the marriage to Cohen, the water Nachum offers serves himself not her. When the Cohens call to confirm the match Libbi moves from reluctance to rejection. She tells Nachum she wants someone else.

Nachum sends Libbi to say goodbye, as she and Nachum return to Antwerp. Neither Akiva nor Libbi express their obvious feelings. Tearfully, Libbi says "Maybe it's for the best. It's easier this way." It's a heart-rending scene: courtship conventions prevent their expression. When Shulem asks who was at the door Akiva says it was his friend Mauricio — the doomed artist he hoped Libbi would prevent his becoming. Now he's real.

When Akiva gives up Libbi and asks for more matches, Shulem turns to Konigsberg's widow Menukha. She has her husband's notebook and frequently advised him. "He always approached it as if it was plumbing. I always said a little psychology might help." She remembers Akiva as "the screw-up. He called it off twice." But (psychology!) she invites Shulem in to talk — and to eat.

The episode's most touching violence is Shoshanna Erblich's suicide. With a fatal disease, she exudes grief. When Malka praises Libbi's beauty Shoshanna says "When I was young I was a lot more beautiful." Stoically, she attributes her tears to allergies: "I never cry. I didn't cry even when my husband kicked the bucket." Then she asks Malka for her painkillers. When Malka cites the Torah's ban against suicide Shoshanna replies: "Who's the *rebbetzin* here, me or you?"

When Malka lists her own reasons to stay alive she can only think of two: to see her off-spiring grown up (they have) and the Torah forbids suicide. Still, she denies Shoshanna her painkillers.

Their conversation is interrupted by schoolgirls coming to sing to the seniors: "The people of Israel live" (!). Inviting requests, they don't know Malka's *Childhood Years*. So Malka and Shoshanna sing it together: The childhood years were so sweet, leaving tender memories, but "Oy, so quickly have I grown old." Time wreaks its own violence, as focused in the rhyme between "childhood years' ("*kindere yoren*") and "grown old" ("*alt gevoren*').

At 2 a.m. Shoshanna phones Malka: she can keep the borrowed nail clipper. (The nails keep growing.) Malka dissuades her from suicide but Shoshanna persists: "Malkele, let me die….Better to die like a

64

rabbi's wife, not a miserable rag." Desiring a dignified death recalls the Inuit ceremony of the first episode.

Shoshanna stops Malka from calling an ambulance. Caressing her hand, Malka promises to stay with her. Malke's wrinkled, thin-skinned hand caressing Shoshanna's bony cold is poetic. In cracking voices they recite the *Shema* together. To fill the void Shoshanna wants the TV on. It's 2 a.m. but there's always news. As the announcer promotes the Jewish survival documentary and the reformed Germany, Shoshanna dies. For both women, the need for compassion and dignity trumps a religious dictate — and converts violence to peace.

That is, we assume Shoshanna dies. We don't see her again. But nor do we see or hear of any funeral. Indeed Germany's rebirth distracts us from her death. Again the drama treats an intimate moment with discretion, respecting privacy. Here death like sex happens off-camera. If we're inclined to condemn Shoshanna for overruling God's lifespan or Malka for not dutifully prolonging her friend's life, this reticence protects us from preferring principle over humanity. That's the driving point of the series. Finally, the possible ambiguity of Shoshanna's suicide supports the possibility of Malka's later.

Episode II, 5

Life as a screw-up (*dafuk*) — that's the central theme here.

Menukha promises Akiva to "find a screw-up just right for you" then proposes one "screw-up *par excellence*." Hard upon this reduction comes Kaufman's news that Akiva just won the Wasserman Award for most promising new artist: a studio, 7,000 shekels a month for a year — and "recognition." Some *dafuk!*

Yet Shulem quips that the award must be from Menukha "for Screw-up of the Year." He reduces the prize to the weekly certificate he gives his students, which provides immediate pride but proves meaningless over time — especially at the Final Judgment! Shulem pretends not to hear Akiva's invitation to the awards ceremony, but then dresses up to attend. "The fact that I have to educate you doesn't mean I'm not proud of you and happy that you're a success."

The two orthodox Jews stick out at the reception, where Kaufman has ordered them kosher plates. The event smacks of assimilation. The Wassermans don't speak Hebrew, so Kaufman translates.Kaufman is directly descended from a rabbi famous for his Biblical text, *The Lion's Roar*. Another attendee left his orthodox roots.

In his ad lib speech Akiva thanks the Wassermans for donating the award, Kaufman for nominating him, his studio neighbour Hadassah Levy for her recommendation — and for bringing the vodka that enables him to speak in public! — and climactically his father "who came here to share my happiness." Shulem corrects that impression. He takes the mike to pitch the Wassermans to donate to his school.

Worse, Shulem denigrates art, the very spirit of the event. Ask an old Jew in his neighbourhood why the gentiles have art and museums, he says, and he'd reply that it's because they don't have the Bible and the study room, respectively. As at the Gottliebs' planning session, Akiva walks out embarrassed by his father. Fortunately, Kaufman and Wasserman are genteel enough to take Shulem's brazen self-service in stride. To Shulem's rejection of their values the company responds with — applause and smiles. But not with any Wasserman money.

Shulem's rudeness validates the Courbet quote used to introduce Akiva: "In our so-civilized society it's necessary for me to live the life of the savage." Akiva and his art are not savage, the speaker notes, but they come from a world "outside our customary discourse." (So is this drama, to its credit and our fascination.)

However selfish Shulem's response to Akiva's success, Nachum's is even worse when Akiva asks Nachum to tell Libbi he won a prize. Nachum says "Congratulations" but he won't tell her. Akiva should never call again.

The other two "screw-ups" are too serious for that term — Giti's and Ruchami's marriages. Shulem brings Giti and Lippe together for one screwed-up marriage to consider the other.

In Zvi Arye's learned view of Jewish law, Ruchami and Hanina must divorce "by benefit of doubt." But Shulem cites another rabbi — to Zvi Arye's indignation. A divorced Ruchami would not be considered unmarried but a divorcee! Having checked out Hanina, Shulem finds him decent: "Perhaps the marriage is not such a bad idea."

Giti stands firm: "I don't care what people say! A 15-year-old can't wake up one morning and get married in a restaurant to the first man she meets." To Giti the restaurant setting is an important element in this screw-up. (Spoiler alert: when Giti will meet Hanina in that restaurant, compassion will finally overcome both context and religious dictate).

Shulem turns the family screw-up to his own purposes. Irritated by Giti's kids, he asks her to suppress her anger at Lippe and to move home. There Giti sets to cleaning up. She rejects Lippe's touch: "I'm only here to get Ruchami back."

At Ruchami's return Giti's anger dissolves: "Now that you're here I only want to hug you." But Ruchami refuses to divorce: "I love my husband." When she corrects Giti — "Nothing was normal around here." — Giti looks pointedly at Lippe: "Maybe things weren't fine here. But that's no reason to run off and get married." Ruchami walks out: "I thought you'd help me. How foolish!"

Lippe is immediately prepared to help his daughter, but Giti refuses. Ruchami "has to realize how absurd it is." Lippe finds the couple an apartment and pays their rent. Later he tells Giti that the couple are not out in the cold. He hears they rented an apartment. "Did you help?" He pauses, reluctant to lie: "Not exactly. Look, Giti, I don't want to fight." He accepts Hanina despite their radical difference in nature: "I never could understand the guys who studied days on end."

Lippe's kindness here is precisely what persuaded Giti to marry him over her parents' objections. As she recalls her introduction to her first suitor, he was a screw-up. Her parents were shocked by his impropriety in bringing her into his car on their first date. Shulem was immediately suspicion: "How does a yeshiva boy get money to have a car?" (He shared it with friends.) Shulem will scold Konigsberg for recommending "a rebel with a car."

The rejected Lippe phoned Giti for a second chance. The screw-up arrived 30 minutes late (not the three he apologizes for) but insisted he's interested only in her. When she stood by her parents' rejection — "We're in different places." — he wished her well and went.

Leaving the hotel, Giti saw that Lippe had given his gloves to the shivering doorman. This kindness converted her. His silly joke (see below) had her laughing helplessly. Seeing Lippe's generosity, she told her parents to complete the match: "I want this man…. He's a good man." She saw beyond the screw-up to his kindness, which he now shows Ruchami and Hanina. In overriding her parents' objections and insisting on her choice of husband, Giti had her daughter's strength.

At the end of the episode Giti brings a blanket to Ruchami's home. Giti's line — "I just don't want you to do anything you'll regret." — is less selfish than Shulem's was: "Don't do anything *we'll* regret."As the apartment recalls Lippe's generosity, Giti invites him back to their bedroom.

However unlike the "rebel with a car," Hanina is also a screw-up. His nonconformity is extreme religiosity. In our first sight of their serene marriage, after their dinner Hanina insists on returning to study: "Only my body is tired. Only my body." He must resume reading because he has been derelict over their first three days of marriage.

As in Giti's renewed marital relations with Lippe, we have no explicit indication that the young couple have consummated their marriage. But we have hints they have and no suggestion they haven't. They are not ignorant of sex. Ruchami has read adult classic fiction, even the forbidden. Having advised her brother on his bedwetting, she knows the plumbing. She first hears Hanina asking God to stop his wet dreams. Perhaps she does. Plus, they are clearly in love. A husband is required to satisfy his wife. Shulem fears her stigmatization as a divorcee, *i.e.*, used. That evidence suggests they are fully wed.

Does it matter? Allowing for but not openly suggesting sex allows a more nuanced treatment of other aspects of the relationship. Were we supposed to consider any other factors — such as *niddah*, the *mikvah*, the *kallah* and *chossen* classes, etc. — they would have been mentioned. They're not so they are irrelevant. These characters have no life, traits, experiences or function outside the frame of this story, beyond its given specifics. They exist only as here detailed. The defence claim of probable consummation rests.

If we're not explicitly told, then the sex doesn't matter here. The new marriage is certainly loving. Ruchami is appalled to see Hanina hold his hand over a flame to wake up. "Find another way. I care for you. I don't want you to be in pain." Hanina is "not used to anyone caring." Ruchami loves watching him study, seeing his visible joy in the beauties of the *Talmud*. She will patiently wait with dinner until he returns. One 3:30 a.m. he finds Ruchami still waiting with their dinner: "It'll serve as breakfast." Ruchami accepts this.

But he doesn't. Hanina has spent the night contemplating their future together — and finds it impossible. "I won't be able to study when you're next to me or when you're waiting for me. I love you too much, Ruchami." He can't focus on the *Talmud* for thinking of her. He will leave — after dinner — for a yeshiva in distant Safed. Shocked, Ruchami now holds a flame to her hand, like Giti's de-numbing iron. Ironically, for all their difference Hanina abandoning Ruchami for his freedom to study recalls Lippe's escape from his family. Hanina flees to discipline, Lippe from it. Abandoning his wife for his study is another example of religion trumping humanity.

And so it goes. Screw-up (*i.e.*, excessively studious) Hanina leaves Ruchami (who supposedly "screwed up" by peremptorily marrying her screwed-up father's antithesis) at roughly the same nocturnal hour that Giti resumes her screwed-up marriage intimacy.

Minor screw-ups enliven the margin. After the award reception Akiva retreats to a felafel stand. When he says to his reflection "You really are a screw-up" the cook takes offence and gives him a black eye. As Menukha consoles him: "Knowing you're a screw-up means you're halfway there." She rejects Akiva's blaming Shulem: "It's very easy to blame your parents for all your problems." And she's been seeing Shulem "from time to time."

Lippe's "silly joke" on his first meeting with Giti is the classic Jewish victim/screw-up story. A punk on a train asks "Who here is named Rabinovich?" One hand goes up. The punk beats the poor man into a broken pile, then leaves. The victim lies there in agony but laughing. "What's so funny?" he's asked. "The joke's on him. My name isn't Rabinovich!"

So, to screw up is human. To make a literature about it — whether an anecdotal joke or a dramatic series — that is so Jewish. That is, so human.

Episode II, 6

Perhaps the central metaphor here is Nachum's curse when he answers the phone and Akiva is silent: "May you swallow an umbrella that opens in your belly. *Amen*!!!" The episode features several such internal afflictions, irruptions physical or emotional. Zvi Arye imputes their religious purpose: illnesses are blessings from God, to test us and our friends' devotion.

When Zvi Arye nips home for lunch he instead finds Tovi listening to the radio declaring domestic duties and motherhood, "the highest form of fulfilment." A friend is getting a kidney transplant from his wife. To test Tovi's devotion Zvi Arye claims the doctors say he needs one. Would she go test for a match?

"All right," Tovi responds, tentatively, "if there's no other option." What if she gets sick? What about the kids? Why the rush? Perhaps the doctors are wrong. They should go to a rabbi and pray.

Her reluctance haunts Zvi Arye. He broaches the issue with Akiva. He asks Menukha if she'd give Shulem a kidney ("Gladly, but I've already donated one to my husband"). When Zvi Arye asks the room who'd give him a kidney several assent but not Tovi. He rushes out, disappointed. She follows in support.

"Your kids are something," Menukha remarks. "And he's the normal one," adds Shulem. The "normal one" gave up his singing ambition at his father's command.

Shulem fails his own relationship test. After five meals Menukha wants to take their relationship "up a notch." Adopting her prey's strategy, she claims that her husband recommended that (if he died) she marry Shulem. He suggests they discuss it in a month. She snatches back his food: "You and your screwed-up brat can park your bums on the sofa all day waiting for the Messiah, for all I care."

Shulem falls. Literally, from a chair while changing a light bulb; effectively, from the grace of his proud independence. Lying helpless, he manages to smoke. Now Dvora lies beside him, recalling when he fell and twisted that foot 20 years ago, dancing with his sons on Purim. She told him to replace those chairs 10 years ago, but he said they were good for another 10. Even when Shulem was right he was wrong. He should not have always denied her desires. Would she now hand him the phone? "I'm dead, Shulem."

Menukha comes to the rescue: "My God, I knew something was wrong. I could feel it!" She had called to say that, as she values spending time with him, he can take longer to consider marriage. Finding him helpless, she takes command. She tends to his foot and feeds him a soup with her own croutons. When Akiva and Zvi Arye find them thus in the kitchen — the Orthodox version of *flagrante delicto* —Shulem sputtering introduces her as his bride.

At the engagement party, Menukha brings him a plate of pasta and insists they renovate the kitchen. Zvi Arye is concerned: "Who is she? Where did she come from?" But the worldlier Lippe is confident: "She'll make him his favourite dishes."

Shulem again turns to Aliza for advice. Having been blessed with such a love as Dvora could he be someone else's husband? Aliza reveals that when she met her present husband she was still in love with another man — Shulem, still unaware. "I put him behind me. I moved on. It was the best decision I ever made." She advises Shulem to "seize with both hands" the chance to marry another fine woman.

On the phone Menukha hears Aliza congratulating Shulem on his engagement. A woman secretary is "inappropriate" — Menukha insists Shulem replace her immediately. Shulem abandons his most loyal supporter. Hiding in his office, he confirms her "coward" (I,2).

The episode opened on a promising note. Shulem compliments Akiva on his omelet which, taken with his painting success, means "I can almost say you're making something of yourself." But he tells Menukha Akiva's prize was "formal approval that being a bum is just fine."

As Farshlufen is going to Antwerp, Akiva gives him a message for Libbi — with a flower. On Farshlufen's phone, Libbi deflects his feelings: "Why talk? What difference would it make?" His proposed visit "would only cause me pain. Please don't phone me again."

In a dream Akiva on the train thinks he sees Libbi ahead but it's not her. Jerusalem metamorphoses into the snows of Antwerp. Another lover feels the deep freeze. In the last scene Akiva joins Shulem at the kitchen table. He awoke wondering if his father is engaged or did he dream it? Akiva's bowl of popcorn suggests that, having lost his love, he's detaching. He'll watch his family's life as if it were a movie.

For all their patriarchal power, the three men seem helpless. Akiva's solitude, Shulem's new marriage and Zvi Arye's marital alienation mark the halfway point in the second season.

Episode II, 7

Before Akiva and Shulem rise from their nadir they must first sink a bit further. In the opening a hammer smashes Shulem's kitchen wall, waking Akiva. He is hurt by Shulem's surprise renovation: "This is Mum's kitchen. Our memory." To appease Menukha Shulem holds fast: "I'm moving on with my life…. Menukha is in charge now. She wants to renovate." When Menukha admits they should have consulted with Akiva, Shulem says no, it's a valuable lesson: "Life is not a picnic." To Shulem a father should add to his children's suffering.

Menukha promises to find Akiva a wife "with both feet on the ground." "I love him like a son. All he needs is a little push, that's all." Shulem's response — "I love him like a son too" — would be funnier if he hadn't so failed his children. Later Shulem suggests Menukha describe Akiva not as an "artist" but as an "Illustrator of books….holy texts" — another lie, disrespectful of his son.

Shulem accedes to Menukha's demands. She wants a huge wedding, at least 200 people, with all their grandchildren, in an expensive hall. He wants a small one, "with a *minyan*" (ten men), no grandchildren. He relents, then rejects her offer to split the hall rental. On the cheques he wants to use the Gregorian calendar dates but surrenders to her Hebrew.

Remembering it's his Dvora's brithday, he begins to reminisce but Menukha cuts him off: "Please, Shulem. We're starting something new. I don't talk about my husband; please don't tell me all about your wife." When she sends him to read on the balcony, Dvora welcomes their tradition of having a brandy on her birthday. Going for the bottle he hears Menukha pitching a client: "Tell your son that celiac is a good thing. His wife will always be thin. I wish I was ciliac." The spell broken, Dvora is gone. Only alone can he set out a glass for her and drink.

Menukha's matchmaking ploys are amusing but with serious import. Elsewhere she hypes the advantages of a husband of "average" height. To make her way in the world the widow must use whatever she has. Like the *rebbetzin*'s currency dealing, Esti's manipulative crying and Giti's capacity for denial, Menukha negotiates with twists and stratagems to make up for women's restriction in the male culture.

To relish his marital memories Shulem has to visit his mother. In a rare political reference, his recalling the couple's annual visits to the Kotel stirs Malka's desire to revisit it. The Kotel is the Wailing (or Western) Wall in Old Jerusalem, one of the Jews' holiest sites. Malka fears the Jordanian snipers that almost killed her husband. She forgets that in the Six Days War Israel took the Kotel back from Jordan.

Shulem walks her to a safe distant view, where she prays for a good wife for Akiva.

Menukha goes too far when she bags Dvora's clothing for charity. She agrees she should have asked him first. Now Shulem stops the renovation: "It's an external thing. I want to focus on the internal." Indeed, the profoundly internal treatment of an external: He rehangs Dvora's clothing. This recalls his weeping over it in I,3. He preserves her memory in the wardrobe, if not in the kitchen. He will close Season Two on another such futile but more destructive sentimentality.

Since moving into his studio Akiva has been unable to paint, to dealer Kaufman's concern. Then a curious incident occurs. At Anshin's, Akiva notices a little boy carrying a goldfish in a plastic bag. Then he's gone. This begins Akiva's mysterious encounter with the phantom Itzikel.

The boy is waiting on the corner for his mother. Akiva brings him to his studio, feeds him (plain) pizza, and amuses him by conversing with the fish. This play recalls his scene with Libbi, riffing on the couple below. This joyous Akiva draws the kid's spontaneous hug. While Itzikel browses through an art book Akiva starts to paint him. He is so focused that he doesn't hear the boy's first request to go to the washroom. On the second, Akiva sends him down the hall. As he leaves, Itzikel lingers over one last look at Akiva. He doesn't return.

When Hadassah brings Akiva her egg salad sandwich she says he has been in the studio all day. He didn't respond to her knocks. She doesn't remember the boy he'd heard her mention. The bench Akiva sat on isn't there. But he has broken through his block and made a painting — of a little boy holding a goldfish in a plastic bag, alone in the world. "Congratulations," Hadassah says, "You painted."

Subconsciously working out an idea for a painting, Akiva moved through his day between the real surrounding and his imagination. He did what that sketchbook in the credits footage embodies: look at the world through his artistic impulse. This imaginative engagement distinguishes the "artist" from the "illustrator of books."

His painting grows out of three elements: Akiva's life, art and religion. From his life comes the loneliness that Shulem's latest banishment has amplified. It recalls motherless Levi Itzhak's heartbreaking solitude. Itzikel (*i.e.*, Little Itzhak.) here is waiting for his mother who doesn't come, sitting on a bench that doesn't exist. His first words are "I am alone." The boy embodies the child's common vulnerability and solitude. Akiva's creativity fuses his own and Levi Itzhak's vulnerability to evoke the archetype of childhood..

The little boy is also a response to the Serov painting of a child's head in Hadassah's studio. This painting that inspired her to become an artist now inspires Akiva. His painting pulls that memory of art into his memories of vulnerability. This work is the "memory of a memory," as he describes the climactic painting in II,12.

Religion provides the painting's third enigma, Itzikel's bag of water with a goldfish. Helpless himself, the boy protects this small packet of helpless life. The fish is the essential animal creature, the essence of life. The water also connotes the *meyim chaim*, the waters of life, also an emblem of the *Torah*.

But the fish is also a specifically Christian symbol. The child thus may also evoke the Christian Messiah, recalling the baptism and cheery baby scene that cast a Christian tone in I,9, where the dream Eran assured Shulem that The Rabbi loves all Jewish sects and Gentiles alike. Akiva's universal abstractions transcend any one religion or sect. Like his motherhood painting in this season's final episode, Akiva's child painting evokes a spirituality that transcends any single faith. He aspires to the universal not sectarian. This combination of life, art and religion is the wholeness Akiva seeks.

Meanwhile, back in reality, Ruchami finds provisions reduced to one onion in the fridge. She phones Hanina for reassurance — but then won't disturb his study. She moves home, to her parents' relief. Again Lippe proves the more sensitive. Ruchami explains that Hanina has moved to Safed: "I'm glad he went. That way no-one will get in the way of his study." Lippe looks on in silent sympathy, but Giti blurts out "I knew this would happen." Lippe turns away helpless.

Giti tells Ruchami to shuck "that ridiculous head covering" that connotes a married woman. But Ruchami takes her marriage vows seriously. Lippe proposes a compromise: she need only wear it outside. She flees a grocery store when she realizes she forgot it. Malevolently, Giti hides it, blaming the boys. Attacking Ruchami's marriage Giti shows none of the character with which she protected hers. With chilling self-unawareness Gitti asks Ruchami "You're married? Where's your husband? Far away?" Safed is closer than Argentina was.

Desperate, Ruchami phones Hanina and has him brought from the study hall: "I had to hear your voice." He dreamt about her last night, studying together at the yeshiva. Responding to her pain, he promises to come home for the weekend.

Through the couple's loving conversation Giti moves in the background, a shadowy threat. Instead of being touched by their obvious love, she despatches Lippe to Safed to abort the visit and demand the divorce. Lippe defends the couple's love but Giti insists: "It's not love, it's fantasy. I hope. When you love someone you don't get up and leave." Lippe proved otherwise, but is too compromised to oppose her. Giti's "fantasy" is how her father dashed his children's aspirations.

Episode II, 8

Two-thirds through the second season Malka dies. But not before she has at least two last salutary effects on her family.

First, she instinctively divides Menukha from Shulem. Malka bristles when Shulem introduces Menukha to her as his new bride. "Who are you?… Your bride. Very nice. Does Dvora know about this?" Menukha bows and scrapes to ingratiate herself. But she ridicules Malka's request to see the sea: "What's so nice about the [smelly] sea?" This Malka takes in silence. But to Menukha's "Life is strong," Malka replies "No, life is very weak." When Menukha pours blessings upon Malka's old age she erupts: "Shut up already, you *klaffte.*" That is, "bitch." The bride departs.

To make amends Shulem brings Menukha flowers (real ones). "Money is no object," says Shulem, before choosing the cheapest. Still angling, Menukha says she likes plastic. To mollify Menukha, Shulem claims his mother has called every woman she ever met a *klaffte.* That lie earns Shulem some of Menukha's ice cream. Later, unwilling to step between those women again, Shulem has Zvi Arye phone to invite Menukha to Malka's funeral.

Malka also teaches Giti to control her pride, lest it control her. Initially Giti insists son Yosa'le attend the famous Tiferet Torah yeshiva, at which Akiva studied. The boy aces his interview, citing a curious law: When a thief modifies a stolen object he is not obligated to return it. When Yos'ale is not accepted Giti tells the principal "You don't have the right not to accept him."

More scrupulous, Lippe refuses Giti's demand he ask an uncle to pressure the yeshiva dean. After reconsideration, the boy is accepted. But Giti now agrees with Lippe's preference for the local yeshiva, which is close to home, with smaller classes, more personal attention, with less pressure on their sensitive son. He'd felt guilty for his rejection: "I guess I didn't pray hard enough." Giti doesn't tell Yos'ale of his acceptance.

Here Giti overcomes the pride that had trumped her son's needs. For that she assumed the assignment Malka's great uncle used: to buy nails at a pharmacy. As Malka taught her, "We can't control everything." This lesson earlier might have prevented the repression that erupted in the fashion store (I,11) and her son's guilt at rejection.

But Malka takes control over her own ending. She arranges to die how and where she wants, with dignity. *Mutatis mutandis*, she dies like an eskimo. Away from her family, she takes a taxi to Tel Aviv and dies on a bench overlooking the sea. She watches young men surfing. A bikini walks by behind her. Amid that secularity she finds a peaceful death alone in nature.

Malka's end is so controlled she may well have followed Shoshanna's example. We don't see her taking the pills. But hints are there. Her coma (I, 12) returned her to Velvale. She knows the technique, saw her friend's painless passage, and —having suffered her dementia and embarrassed aftermath — may well have reached Shoshanna's resolve. Malka, after all, had herself found only two reasons to live on. The *Rebbetzin* provided a pass on the ban. Asked "How did she die?" Shulem replies "Only God knows (II,9). Again, we appreciate the drama's reticence and the richness ambiguity allows.

Though Akiva is not involved in his grandmother's narrative here, he frames the episode. The first scene establishes the double sacredness in his life. Kaufman says Akiva's Itzikel "reminds me of me." Like the motherhood painting in II,12, here a particular portrays a universal. That leads Kaufman to his lesson. When the boy used to fall asleep at *shule*, his grandfather taught him: "The synagogue is a sacred place. You shouldn't sleep in a sacred place." So is the studio, Kaufman asserts, "a sacred place," not to be slept in.

Homeless, Akiva accepts Hadassah's invitation to stay in her parents' guest cottage. She grew up in that Jerusalem suburb and is "still growing there." So might Akiva.

The setting is idyllic, indeed an Eden where Akiva can work in peace. *En route* he tells Hadassah that his neighbourhood feels completely strange since his love departed. Whether he means Elisheva or Libbi, "It [worked out] but she left." She invites him to a kosher dinner, to meet her parents, but he declines. Instead he takes a photo album glimpse into the woman's early life. Hadassah *Levy*'s family is a healthier version of a Jewish family than *Levi* Itzhak, in parental presence as well as in the proud support of art and the woman's freedom.

Hadassah finds him painting serenely. "It's as if an air conditioner in my head has suddenly been turned off." The peace is disturbed by jackals braying at nightfall, but there is magic there. Hadassah shows Akiva how her father taught her to silence them: extend your arms and concentrate. "But you have to do it with me, so it works…. I thought it was crazy too, but it always works." The jackals would cease braying on their own. But humans crave the delusion of power over nature. Here as in art, Akiva finds the supernatural in the real world, the spiritual in the material. He's empowered and calmed.

As Akiva and Hadassah paint each other's portraits their comfort augurs intense connection. Then Akiva realizes that he has for the first time forgotten to say his morning prayers. He rushes home. As Hadassah ponders his touching portrait of her, we recall his loving drawing of Elisheva and that dashed romance.

Living at the Levys', with Hadassah (the name of the American Zionist Women's Organization), Akiva has the opportunity to live a kosher Jewish life outside his stricter community, and to develop as an artist. When Akiva drops in on Hadassah's studio (II,7) she is praying. But at his first lapse from orthodoxy he flees her Eden.

Malka's death also brings reconnections. In his grief, Shulem, phones Aliza, to report his loss and that he won't be at work tomorrow: "I know you're there to look after the school." She reminds him he fired her. Weeping, Shulem says "Aliza, good tidings"

The funeral also brings back Nachum and Libbi. At the door Nachum extends his hand but Shulem goes for the full forgiving hug: "That's that. Mum's dead." "Where is everybody?" Libbi asks, meaning Akiva. "He's disappeared," Shulem explains. "Off the face of the earth. Into his painting." Since resuming his art Akiva "forgot who he is" — *i.e.*, discovered it.

Shulem breaks with Menukha over her advice on dealing with Aronovsky, "The Elderly Whisperer." This hustler records videos of seniors reminiscing over their lives, which he sells to their survivors. "I have regards from your late mother," he begins, then describes the two-hour tapes he will provide for $990. "A man's got to live." He has an instalment plan.

Aronofsky raises moral issues of Talmudic subtlety. On the spectrum of artists here, he stands between the idealist Sasha and the fake Fuchs. As Akiva will attempt, Aronofsky is performing a "sacred job," even if his merely recording life ranks below Akiva's imaginative conceptualizing. In Judaism memorializing the dead is a sacred responsibility. Here at least three moral issues arise.

First is Aronofsky. Can something be a "good deed," leave alone "a sacred job," if the intention is corrupt? Aronofsky's "sacred" function is undermined by his greed. Though he drops his video charge from $990 to $700, has not his fee contaminated his product? Moreover, he is predatory, popping up at *shivas* to prey on the mourning. Don't his motive and strategy negate his *mitzvah*? In his sanctimonious self-service Aronofsky is the art version of Shulem and Nachum.

Then there's Menukha's dilemma. Should she intercede and how far? She has already assumed — indeed, overstepped —some wifely responsibilities, like ordering the kitchen reno and having Shulem fire his most faithful friend. Here she advises Shulem haggle down the con's price. But how caring is her advice? Having told Shulem not to reminisce about Dvora, she'd hardly want a Malka video around, especially given their first meeting. Her advice is wholly self-serving.

Then there is Shulem's dilemma. A video of his mother speaking and dancing would be as "priceless" to him as his proud gravesite. Need the artist's corrupt motive spoil that treasure? He can afford it, especially since becoming principal, so why balk even at the original price? Why sacrifice such a treasure over the maker's motive? It still shows his Malka alive, even reminiscing over his birth and naming.

When Aronofsky calls to negotiate, Shulem is ready to pay the $700 but Menukha intervenes. Her $100 price is an insult for the time spent recording Malka and the fact this is both Aronofsky's creative idea and his livelihood. She calls Aronofsky's erasure threat a bluff.

"Who's the *klaffte* in the background?" Aronofsky asks, channelling Malka. Shulem hangs up. When he relents and phones back, the tape has been erased. Shulem let Menukha monetize his mother's memorial. That is his responsibility not hers.

But he blames her. Shulem phones to tell Menukha not to come to the funeral: "I think I made a mistake.... I just realized we're not suited.... We're not getting married.... Take care." Unlike his twice maligned son, Shulem is responsible for cancelling his engagement. He lacks the courage to do it in person.

In the final scene, as Akiva returns home for his *tefillin* he passes a poster announcing his grandmother's death. The nearly-missed funeral completes his fall from Hadassah's Eden. In front of those posters, Akiva extends his arms — summoning Hadassah's magic power to ward off the wild. Here —and alone — it won't work.

As if a presiding grace, Libbi watches him from his balcony.

Episode II, 9

This episode is about loss: Malka's *shiva,* the surprise in her will, Ruchami's loss of Hanina, Akiva's sacrifices to win Libbi. As with Aronofsky's tape, every loss raises questions of responsibility.

At Malka's *shiva*, Shulem and Nachum grow impatient with the ritual condolences. While Shulem nods off, Nachum grows irritable, insulting one visitor, scolding Akiva for drawing. One commiseration recurs: "We're in God's hands." Life and death, blessing and affliction, all's in God's hands. Man is powerless. "We know nothing."

But in the main plot-lines — Giti undermining Ruchami's marriage, Libbi demanding Akiva's submission — the characters' suffering is entirely due to human action. Apart from Malka's death, all this suffering is due to man's righteousness. The Rubik's Cube may seem incongruous among Malka's *tchachkes,* but the secular diversion embodies the complex alignment needed for this family's integrity.

Shulem calls art dealer Kaufman "Just a guy who pays [Akiva] to paint. A secular man with a guilty conscience." But Nachum curses him: "Damn those evil people," *i.e.*, the secular. Nachum summons divine force to serve his prejudice.

Left on their own, Libbi and Akiva show a comfortable intimacy. Shulem despatches Akiva to make his own inventory of Malka's possessions, because he doesn't trust his brother. Libbi jokes that Nachum told her to "hide the diamonds." He proves that larcenous.

In a more momentous discovery, finding Velvale's *tallis* and *tefillin* prompt Akiva to tell Libbi about that day when he was so involved in painting that he forgot his morning prayer. Now she questions the compatibility of art and religion. "How did that happen?" She worries about his two-week tour of American galleries and museums that Wasserman has offered. Where will Akiva stay, eat, pray? Why does he even want to go abroad? "I've always lived abroad. I guess I just want to be here." She ends on the root of her concern: "Don't forget your *tefillin*."

Libbi tells Nachum she wants to marry Akiva but under her conditions. To the "prodigal son" Nachum conveys her acceptance, though he would "prefer someone more serious, more God-fearing…. You're a good kid. Just a little confused. You're a bohemian artist. Not crazy but you live a crazy life."

Libbi's conditions are simple: Akiva has to give up his self. He must completely abstain from painting, exhibitions, and any traveling. Yet he must run Nachum's new travel agency in Jerusalem. Akiva must pray thrice daily in a *minyan*, never to forget his morning prayers and to raise their children on the Torah. While he contemplates these terms, he may not speak to Libbi before *shabbes*.

Libbi's conditions are a far cry from her initial response to Akiva's art: "If God had given me such a gift, such a talent, I'd do my best not to waste it" (II,2). Without knowing about Hadassah, she fears losing Akiva to the artist's life. Hence her severe demands.

Akiva accedes. He leaves Kaufman a phone message cancelling the trip and exhibition. As for his studio paintings, "Do what you want with them. I want no part." He'll not discuss this further.

Giti also abandons her better nature to fend off a perceived threat. With Lippe off to cancel Hanina's visit and force a divorce, Giti shows Ruchami a face of warm acceptance. "I miss him so much,"

Rychami confides. "That's nice," Giti smiles, duplicitously. Still, she sternly insists she can't buy a new dress during *shiva*.

Lippe can't stand up to Giti. Against his conviction he agrees to take the long trip to Safed. At the yeshiva he finds Hanina absorbed in his study. Why is he soaking his feet in ice water? Ruchami told him to find an alternative to burning his hand to stay awake. His obeying his wife is healthier than Lippe's.

Lippe begins friendly, apologizing for having hit Hanina at their first meeting. Then he turns cold: "You won't be coming for *shabbes*.... You're not wanted in our house. You must forget our daughter." Worse, like that other ignoble patriarch Shulem, he lies: Ruchami "never wants to talk to you again. She realizes she made a mistake and wants nothing to do with you.... I promise you, this is what she wants." Hanina must appear in court and agree to a divorce. "I'm sorry," Lippe says, genuinely but ineffectually.

Gitti maintains her false acceptance. She tells Ruchami how beautiful she looks anticipating Hanina's arrival. She smiles at Ruchami's "He's so righteous he doesn't care what I wear. But it matters to me." Giti pretends understanding even as she destroys her daughter's bliss. "I am being honest," she claims. We see Ruchami's painful wait at the bus stop.

These two ostensibly loving betrayals — Giti's and Libbi's — are connected by a three-scene montage. After Lippe leaves Hanina we see the boy despondent, then Ruchami mending her dress for his visit, then Kaufman and Akiva finishing his visa application and toasting his US trip. Standing outside the gallery, Libbi sees the men, feels excluded from their world and sets her course. Rather than join Akiva's celebration she goes to give her father her demands to abort his career.

Both plots show parents stifling their children's lives. Though Libbi overrides her father's objection to Akiva she uses him to enforce her conditions. Giti uses Lippe to keep Hanina from Ruchami. That may be the distinction between the two similar lies the fathers make to destroy their offspring's romance. Shulem lied to Elisheva saying Akiva didn't want to see her again. Now Lippe tells Hanina that Ruchami doesn't want to see him. Lippe's lie is not as extreme as Shulem's. Lippe says Ruchami agrees to the end of her marriage, which is true insofar as reluctant submission can be considered agreement. While neither lie may be defensible, Shulem's lie is a destructive assertion of his power, while Lippe — his own adventure having compromised his authority in his marriage — acts in submission to Giti's.

Here both destructive authority figures are women. If the drama overall exposes patriarchal authority — especially in Shulem's ruinous rule — here the destructive domination is by women. That is, a matriarchy could be as inhumane as a patriarchy is. The problem is systemic oppression not gender.

Malka's will is notable on two counts. In its formal opening, Malka identifies herself by her descent from her father, with no mention of her mother. This is the religion's historically patriarchal structure, which continues in contemporary orthodoxy (and is rejected by the Reform movement).

Malka's will is read between Lippe giving Giti Hanina's personal journal and Giti conveying it to Ruchami. Like the will, the journal is a message from the lost. The emotion Ruchami finds in Hanina's testament makes the legal document seem shabby.

Malka's will is expected to divide everything equally between her two sons. As Shulem reads it aloud he chokes on one term: Malka bequeathes her apartment to Nachum. The rest both sons share.

Shulem is jolted. His son Zvi Arye has lived in that flat, rent-free, since Malka went into the seniors' residence. Malka's will renders the penurious Zvi Arye homeless — and Shulem feeling betrayed for his years of caring for her. Nachum explains that Malka probably wrote that will when he had just gone bankrupt and she was trying to help him. She'd neglected to rewrite it.

Magnanimously, Nachum announces Libbi's engagement to Akiva and gives them the flat. That still leaves Zvi Arye out in the cold. As we've heard continually: Well, what can we do. It's all in God's hands. God took Malka before she could rewrite the will. We know nothing and can do nothing.

Of course, the issue here is rather what people do to when not for each other, not what any divinity inflicts upon them. Malka not God wrote and left unamended her will. Nachum not God gives "his" flat to his Libbi — evicting Zvi Arye. Libbi decides what Akiva will do with his God-given talent. Giti overrules Ruchami's marriage.

Shulem ruined Zvi Arye's life and falsely claimed to be paying six mortgages, leaving his most thwarted son unhoused.

This may be the function of the "Minsk Melody." In Shulem's first dream here, his mother hums it while she knits with a stream of audio tape (!) and reminisces with Dvora about dancing at her wedding. She attributes the song to Shulem's famous great great grandfather. But in his waking life nobody has heard of this famous "Minsk Melody." Malka later sings Shulem to sleep with it.

In fact, Shulem creates this melody in the dream. Knitting with audio tape surreally turns the material of recording into creation. In context, this song is another instance of someone attributing his own creation to an earlier authority. Shulem thinks the song preexists him but it's the product of his own imagination — like the various laws and conventions for which people claim divine orders to afflict others. The melody is his unconscious creation, as his stories supporting his position are his conscious ones, a.k.a. lies.

Episode II, 10

Aliza provides a pivot for this episode when she tells Shulem why she won't return to work for him: "Once you make up your mind stick with it. The worst thing is to choose one thing and to want another." Working for Shulem would remind her that she'd futilely loved him. Shulem is a past not to be regretted. The major characters live with their hard choices, whatever their abandoned alternatives.

Shulem is dissatisfied with secretary Farshlufen. Aliza has to tell him to use water not soda on the plants. Shulem finds him sleeping through a phone ringing at his desk, then absent: "He stayed in bed instead of sleeping here."

Shulem opts out of his New Orphan Blues when he adopts Aliza's cure for her same depression: The Gashash Trio's comedy recordings. This exposes him to a new technology: "Do you sell tape recorders to play the CDs too?" He can't leave the old behind.

Some of their jokes reflect Shulem's secular issues, such as the cut from an Akiva-Libbi art discussion to the comedian's punchline: "I can't use acrylic if I'm not in the mood" [*laughter*]. When Aliza points out that he's accidentally playing the comedy on the school PA system Shulem is embarrassed. The principal should not be beaming anything secular into the school, especially such "pure nonsense." "No harm done" he assures himself. As a president may use "Believe me" to cover a major lie, Shulem uses "No harm done" to cover his greatest humiliations (here, as when courting Adi).

As Elana Horwitz points out, the sign in Shulem's office declares that people who feel the sweetness of Torah need nothing else, "for the Torah contains all the goodness in the world." Perhaps sometimes there is a need for some nonsense.

Shulem lies to Aliza by reflex: "I was listening to the radio." No, he'd deliberately put on his CD. He lied when he told Aliza he had to fire her for budgetary reasons. Now he admits the truth — after another lie: "I didn't fire you…. My bride didn't want me to have a woman secretary." He claims to have defended Aliza strenuously but we saw him immediately cave. Powerful Shulem is weak and false.

Libbi and Akiva struggle over his abandoning art. Surprisingly, Libbi suggests he do a drawing for their wedding invitations. She doesn't want him to stop completely: "Painting here and there is nice."

Akiva's "surprise" date, going skating, is an emblem of their relationship. They're skimming an icy surface, where Libbi is in control and comfortable but Akiva is out of his element, tottering, falling, but eventually finding a balance. Walking home, Libbi jokes about not having to change her name — unless she opts for Libbi Shtisel-Shtisel, or puts the other Shtisel first. That's arbitrary, like her demands of him.

At Kaufman's ambush Akiva stands firm but evasive: "I need some peace and quiet." Kaufman eschews the Art argument for the practical: Akiva's commitments to him. Kaufman rang up expenses for his exhibition. "You got money, a studio, you can't just walk away." He threatens to sue him. Akiva walks away.

When Libbi sees Akiva's invitation drawing and hears how he enjoyed drawing again, that he misses the activity, even the smell of charcoal she reconsiders her ban. "Everything has a smell" to the alert artist. To bolster her resistance she meets secretly with Kaufman to explain her concerns.

Kaufman is gracious: "Congratulations. My grandparents were cousins too." Akiva has to drop art, she says, "so he can live his life the way he wants to live it." Of course, that's her choice not his. Kaufman denies self-interest: "I care about his talent."

This conversation reveals a new side of Nachum's character. In the first scene here Nachum is the stereotypical hustler. He instructs manager Akiva: "No need to be nice to anyone. Those damn evil people" — *i.e.*, his secular clients. Just "Identify the person" in a few seconds: figure how much money they have, then pitch the appropriate package. Nachum is the travel agent version of Aronofsky (II,8).

Untrustworthy himself, Nachum trusts no-one. He delayed opening a Jerusalem travel office — modestly named Nachum Tours — until he had someone he could trust, *i.e.*, a son-in-law. He installed an HD security camera, not at the security company's insistence, as he claims, but because he likes to watch his employees when he's bored. Libbi learns how to turn it off, to spare Akiva the spying eye.

Nachum's shady dealings have left him in financial difficulty. Four major airlines block his business until he makes a substantial payment. "Damn evil anti-semites," he declares them. When he surprises Shulem with a late visit, bearing scotch and pastry, Shulem infers his brother needs help. As "a small favour" Shulem should borrow 100,000 shekels. Nachum has made small errors on "red tape, forms." He can't go to his usual guarantor "because of some nonsense in the past." The vagueness confirms his shiftiness.

Shulem agrees on the condition that Nachum sign a form. It's not an IOU but Nachum's admission that he neglected their mother for 15 years. Nachum initially refuses to "sign this nonsense" but with no other option relents. Shulem gives Nachum the signed statement. For Shulem it was a matter of personal principle, using his power to humiliate his brother, as he did Akiva for that morning off school.

Nachum finagles free advertising for his new company. He promises a senior rabbi he will honour his deceased mother by commissioning a new Torah. It will be ready in a year, he says, but he requests a large ad now thanking him — and his new travel agency — for the donation. This is another personal exploitation of religion. Nachum thanks the rabbi with a reflexive tirade: "I'll show those damn evil people…. The gentiles, the enemy of the Jews." Nachum dismisses all the secular as *Reshaim Arurim*, damn evil people. Religion is his front for rapacity.

After this satiric characterization, we're surprised when Libbi reveals her father's ardour for classical music. He was especially enchanted by Mahler's *Fifth Symphony*, a passion which the secular Kaufman shares. In naming it "the tragic symphony," Kaufman mistakes it for the *Sixth*. This is not the scriptwriter's mistake but the secular authority's: No-one is perfect. Nachum often played this music for Libbi. Once when she asked for it he'd erased it. He'd replaced Mahler with a lengthy recording of silence.

Libbi feels Akiva must abandon art for the same reason Nachum gave up Mahler: "Sometimes you feel something is pulling you in. A Jew has to know where to stop before he drowns and can't get out." This could be anyone's explanation for withdrawing from any commitment. Specifying "a Jew" cites the people's historical persecution and consequent insecurity. Fear inhibits risk or commitment.

The episode closes on the men's alternative responses to self-denial. Akiva surrenders his self by turning the security camera back on. We watch him pace in his father-in-law's cage. He bows like a deferential performer. Then he shreds his wedding invitation drawing, to complete his denial of art.

In the last shot, Nachum stands on the balcony listening to — and with cigarette in hand conducting — Mahler's *Fifth Symphony*. Here the vulgar businessman outshines his respectable brother, who shows nothing like this passion for anything. The shady businessman remembers the culture he sacrificed. We — if not he — wonder what he might have been had he allowed himself his sensitivity.

A pertinent irony lies in Nachum's and Menukha's names, which connote consolation, peacefulness, rest. Yet both are driven, upsetting figures. They destroy Shulem's peace and rest and lose their own. The Mahler scene suggests why the writers gave those destructive characters those ill-fitting names: they do not live up to their potential better nature.

The torn, embittered Nachum may also prefigure an Akiva who had forsworn his self. Shredding his drawing suggests Akiva would not enjoy any recovery of his lost passion, as Nachum revisits here.

Episode II, 11

As Shulem's "old Yiddish saying" has it, "A Jew with a dog — either he is not a Jew or it is not a dog."

If that observation were just descriptive, it would be fine. Perhaps on a *per capita* basis fewer Jews have pets. Who knows or cares? But Shulem uses it as a proscription, to correct his grandson's saving the abandoned puppy. The Jew is forbidden to have a dog. A Jew is disqualified for having a dog. This is problematic.

However playful, the adage makes an ill-founded definition of what constitutes a Jew — or humanity, or virtue. A Jew is a Jew whether there's a dog or not. The dog is a dog whoever is with it. Renaming or recategorizing does not alter its nature.

Also, a Jew and a dog are two of God's creatures. On the scale of souls they share at least the *nefesh* awareness of the physical world. Pet-lovers also share the *ruach* of emotions, if not the higher *neshumah*. Declaring either "an impure animal" is to impose a human prejudice against one (or two) of God's creations. The impurity is the prejudice, not the creature.

What's in a name? Everything and nothing. The theme of this episode is the question of identity and the perils of compromising it. This issue is imperative for all the major characters.

Dreading her divorce, Ruchami reminds Lippe of his *Bat Mitzvah* advice: "You know you're doing the right thing when your heart is happy." Lippe says he's sorry about the impending divorce, but "I guess it's the right thing to do." Her aching heart tells Ruchami it isn't. The emotions prove the proper guide for the personal dilemmas in this episode. "Hanina's wife" is now her proper identity.

When Yosa'le is expelled from the yeshiva for taking a little dog in from the rain, he and not the yeshiva official is the true Jew, *i.e.*, the caring soul. The boy's compassion shames his grandfather's jocular adage and the yeshiva's ban. What makes a better *mentsch* (good human being) cannot make a worse Jew.

The dog is named Dubche, which Annie Attali says is Polish for "little behind." It's apt: cute but denigrating. Ironically, the name parallels that other vagabond stray in need of compassion, Lippe (the name suggesting someone from the Polish village Lipa, tinged with the sourness of the lime).

At first Shulem disdains of the secular people who care for stray mutts. But he shares his grandson's shock that the pound could "put [him] to sleep" if he's unclaimed in three weeks. The euphemism is an evasion of responsibility, like the adage. With the boy back at the school, Shulem promises to get Dubche "a five star accommodation." But the mutt's friendliness erodes Shulem's resistance. Having recoiled from the dog, he stoops to pet him.

In part because he doesn't have any, Shulem does not give Dubche dog food. At his most humane, Shulem doesn't treat him like a dog. He gives him a plate of meat and potatoes, then later some leftover *shabbes* chicken schnitzel. Two of God's creatures share food without prejudice. This is Shulem at his uncharacteristic best. With this sensitivity Shulem might have better nourished himself and his family.

When Shulem returns to the empty flat he's worried when Dubche doesn't respond to his calls. Dubche must have left through the front door, which Shulem glancingly finds ajar. One of the most common concerns on the Facebook chat lines is "What happened to the dog?" The writers failed to tell us. Speculation abounds.

Now, if we're not told what happened to Dubche then we don't need to know. It's irrelevant. The dog — like all the other characters and all the physical props — has no existence or character other than what is given within this story. He came, he served his purpose, that's all. As Itzikel with the fish popped up in Akiva's life — on whatever level — Dubche popped up in Yosa'le's. He gave the yeshiva boy one last reminder that humanity towards God's creatures should override even religious rules. Yosa'le here shows a finer humanity than in his absolutist criticism of Ruchami (I,11). His grandfather needs this lesson even more.

But there's a reason we *should* not know Dubche's fate. A good deed is a good deed regardless of what may happen later. Knowing Dubche's future might cloud the issue. Did he live to 120 as a support dog? Did he catch rabies and attack a kindergarten class? Regardless of the future, saving him was the right thing to do. To preserve the virtue of his rescue, Dubche's fate is not disclosed.

Of greater consequence, Giti doesn't know who Hanina is when he drops by her restaurant, on his way to the Rabbinical Court for his divorce. They connect because neither knows who the other is. They meet without predisposition (as Rabbi Cheshin counseled in I,5).

Giti is immediately drawn to the boy's earnestness and sensitivity. After all, she *is* her daughter's mother, even though her stern role disrespects her daughter's feelings. To this strange sensitive boy Giti responds from her heart. She gives Hanina meatballs and potatoes, as her father feeds his stranger, the "dog."

Nor did Giti know Hanina when she judged him. She "knew" only the monster she imagined seduced her helpless daughter. When Ruchami dreads seeing him at the divorce court Giti assumes she fears his rage. "Just goes to show you've never met him," Ruchami says. Seeing him just to part from him is what "will be too painful."

We don't know why — out of all the kugel joints in Geula — Hanina picks Giti's restaurant for lunch. By chance? Divine intervention? We are, after all, in God's hands. Or because in its previous life, as Anshin's cafe, this is where Hanina and Ruchami were married? For the dreaded end of his marriage he returns to where it started. So much has changed, in his life and marriage as in the restaurant. All are now in Giti's hands. But Hanina felt an instinct to return.

The boy asks for what lunch he can get for his last nine shekels. He rejects Giti's offer to let him repay the difference on his next visit. He may not return to Jerusalem. Losing Ruchami, why would he?

Giti devises a face-saving deal: the nine-shekel special, a full entree with dessert. Her affection deepens when he says his mother used to make him that dish, that she died a week before his *Bar Mitzvah.* She had him wear his new suit for her in advance, so it would not be "new" for his ceremony, during her *shiva.* That shames Giti for refusing Ruchami a new dress. His mother's generosity stirs Giti: "You can eat here whenever you want. On the house."

As the Weisses wait outside the divorce court, Lippe doubts Hanina: "I hope he remembers to come. He probably forgot." Ruchami knows: "He said he'll be here so he'll be here. You'll see." Hanina ascends to the challenge (from a lower floor). He and Ruchami steal compulsive glances. When Giti recognizes the boy she goes off to think, then calls Lippe over, leaving the couple alone.

We're not shown what then happens. This is another deliberate ellipsis, reminding us that the life here overflows the narrative frame. The episode closes on the Weiss family with their son-in-law enjoying a happy dinner at home. Which is even better than on the house. The shot frames the expanded family tightly to emphasize their intimacy.

That homey scene contrasts to the restaurant scene where Lippe plays rich man, a "*macher*," before telling Giti his investment of Renta's payment has put 287,000 shekels into their bank account. Lippe orders a 1,050-shekel bottle of "Hamburger," a.k.a Teperberg Port, but Giti insists on a 100-shekel wine.

Fortunately, Lippe drops this swagger, which has tempted him from his courting days, driving his shared car, to the liberties of Argentina. He lets Giti decide how to use the money. Hence the restaurant by which Giti makes Lippe the entrepreneur he has wanted to be. Having overridden Giti's will to get the money, now he leaves to her its use. First with the wine choice, then with the business, Lippe gives her the authority his culture gives him.

When Lippe invested Renta's payment with a community broker, I was probably not alone in expecting his complete loss of that money, even his defrauding. We're used to seeing such urgent gambles fail. And what investment wisdom would we expect in a community that is not just unworldly but anti-worldly? And where Nachum is our closest business acquaintance? In Lippe's investment success this community meets its members' needs.

Giti's and Lippe's reform recall Shulem's other "saying": "Every Jew has to grow up sometime." Why the "Jew"? The people's history puts them on constant alert. And "grow up" means what?

Is Akiva's "growth" the maturing that Nachum brags he achieved in 30 minutes, that Shulem failed to in 27 years? That growth is rather submission, like his finding himself was Shulem's "lost himself" (II,9). When Shulem learns the harsh conditions Nachum claims to have set he urges Akiva not "to give in to Nachum's every whim." To thwart his brother Shulem finally supports his son. As for Libbi, "You think your mother knew every thing I did?"

At his father's suggestion, Akiva will satisfy Kaufman's lawyer by exhibiting under an assumed name. From Kaufman Akiva learns the respectable term: "pseudonym." For this compromise Kaufman reduces the additional paintings required of Akiva from six to one.

That one is pivotal. Akiva starts to paint: a few lines, shapes, but with no Fuchsian photo to direct or to restrict him. Akiva smokes and paints. The result: a woman holding a baby.

As with Itzikel, this work grows out of an other-worldly experience. Akiva dreams of his mother — the industrious Dvora — sewing. She doesn't recognize him; he forgets his own name. She is sewing his initials on his *tefillin* bag. So he has lost his identity, not she her memory. To recover it, Akiva tells Kaufman he will show under his own name. As denying one's name is denying one's self, so is an artist's denial of art.

After Akiva tells Libbi about his dream, she describes her last night's nightmare. She and her parents are on a rattling fast train but it runs on water not on rails. Her father announces that the train is too heavy so some people will have to be thrown overboard. Unknowingly, she has intuited the couple's precariousness. She empathizes with Akiva's fear of losing his identity, but she rejects its defence. Her nightmare confirms their underlying harmony. As expressions of their subconscious, both dreams are truer to their natures than their waking postures are.

At his studio Akiva shows her the painting that — against their agreement — he has just made. He realizes he was wrong to give up his art. He assumed that (as Nachum brags) Nachum imposed those conditions. "Why would you ask that of me? It's in my soul. This is who I am. This is whom you love." The ban mast have been "your father's whim. It's not you." But it is her, she insists. His being an "artist" would imperil her dream of a secure Jewish home.

What's in a name, in a word? In the opening scene, Anshin's customers mourn his closing of his restaurant. He's only moving, but "Leaving the neighbourhood is closing shop." That's a question of "naming." The shop has "closed," it has "moved" — contradictory terms cover the same reality and effect. In any case, Giti takes over the space and has it repainted in a "warmer and cleaner" white. It works.

Naming can be a problem. It sets the *Talmud* scholars debating hairline distinctions until, for example, they come up with the resolution — as firm as it is arbitrary — that "food that is one third done cannot be cooked any further." How precise is that "one third"? As precise as the other rule's "Jew" and "dog"?

Zvi Arye has a more profound conflict over his identity. He resists an invitation to sing in a band: "A scholar like me a wedding singer?" Which is he? Tovi encourages him: "Aren't you fed up with thinking about what other people will think?" Besides, "being a singer is very dignified." Indeed singers are more honoured than Torah scholars. Plus, they need the money. In a minor key, she washes the "disposable dishes" because dishes should not be demeaned and dismissed just because they're named "disposable."

Zvi Arye descends the stairs to his audition. In the "OK or Oy Vey" test he earns a hearty OK. He performs like a professional, but to protect his family he— as Akiva is tempted to do — adopts a pseudonym, Arye Cohen.

His chosen song puts a religious context on the theme of hidden identity. *Even in Concealment* proclaims that "Even in the most concealed places, Certainly He of the blessed name is also found." That is, God is everywhere, behind whatever name or identity, behind every concealment. As the self survives any cover. When he sings this song to Tovi the lyric turns into romantic commitment:"I stand with you. Even through hard times that may befall, I stand, I stand, I stand." In all creatures of whatever name or identity God and this true believer will stand firm. For man as for dog.

Though he balks at turning pro, "Arye Cohen" accepts the job offer, *i.e.*, his new but personally rooted identity. "You want to be a singer or not?" "Yes. It's been my lifelong dream." That trumps the ambition he expressed to Tovi, to be a head teacher — like his father.

His new identity revives the romance in Zvi Arye's marriage. After he obliges Tovi's request for a song she invites him to "come to sleep. It's late." (Earlier she went to bed without him.) Checking his watch, he pauses for a smile of anticipation, then follows. Sending him to a late rehearsal, she promises to wait up — but he must wake her if she dozes off. Picking up on this romance, at the rehearsal Zvi Arye celebrates the voice of joy as love between a groom and his bride.

Over smokes outside, band leader Gurelnick compares him to the well-known singer Zicherman. "Zicher" is Yiddish for "certain," which Zvi Arye is not. Zicherman was a serious Torah scholar who became so hooked on the stage that he dropped his studies, shucked *yarmulke* and sidelocks, left his grey wife with "that pathetic head covering," indeed forsook his family to be a star in Tel Aviv. This rebel won the lottery Sucher lost.

"A man of weak character," Zvi Arye observes. "I don't know," Gurelnick remarks. Whether the rebel acted out of strength or out of weakness depends on who does the naming. The name reveals the namer more than the named. That's the perspective lesson from Shulem's astronomy class (I,7).

Zvi Arye's predicament is not unusual. Indeed, the *Nu? Nu?* song (I,8) is by cantor Pinchas Segal who performed folk songs as Pierre Pinchik. The song comes from an album, *The Two Sides of Pinchik*, one side Pinchik pop, the other Segal religious. He didn't have to choose between his two musical cultures, but assumed different names for his different musical identities. Zicherman's success/failure warns Zvi Arye he may have to.

Back home Zvi Arye beams at his sleeping Tovi — in grey. He leaves the band: "It's a personal matter. I can't." Tovi awakens with a start: "What's wrong?" "Nothing, praise God. Let's go to bed."

While Akiva risks losing Libbi to preserve his true self, Zvi Arye recoils from the risk in his true ambition. With a family now, his choice is harder than when he was a bachelor. Rather than risk temptation he retreats to security. At least he proved he is still a singer — if he chooses. If this time the decision is his, not his father's, he is still paying for Shulem's oppression. As is Tovi. Zvi Arye's decision may not sit so well with her. She just dreamed he sang in a big concert.

Episode II, 12

The drama's conclusion is framed by wedding preparations, first literal, then implicit. By the old saw, comedies end in weddings and tragedies start with them. By closing on the healthy lovers instead of on the mad Shulem the season ends upbeat.

The episode opens on a row of white wedding gowns, where Giti prepares Ruchami for her formal ceremony. The scene emphasizes the religious ban against the couple seeing or speaking to each other in the week before their wedding. At the end Libbi joins Akiva on a bench in the Vittorio Veneto, an 18th Century Italian village synagogue preserved in the Jerusalem Museum. Their marriage will admit his art to their religion as the museum accommodates the synagogue.

The two plot lines are closely paralleled. "Maybe we have to forgive," Ruchami writes Hanina, with respect to his severance from his father. We hear Ruchami's love letter to Hanina over separate shots of the divided Akiva and Libbi: "I ask myself why the people we love the most hurt us the most."

The loss of Dvora (I,i) echoes in Hanina's explanation that "When my mother died it was as if I'd passed with her." He rejected his father for remarrying — as advised to, for his kids' sake —four months after her funeral. Hanina had drifted until he found a vacant synagogue with a spare room, a *Talmud* and a study space. Both couples here find their love in vacated synagogues, the unused shell of formal religious service — a positive form of the *Klippah* (II,3). The spirit of union survives even absent religious services.

Hanina won't invite his father for fear of painful rejection. Touched at Lippe reading to his son, Ruchami takes the initiative and phones to invite Hanina's father to their wedding. He welcomes their engagement: "I've been praying for Hanina three times a day for years." Now he will pray for her too. After promising to bring Hanina's siblings to the wedding, he fails to collect the invitation. To Lippe Ruchami wonders "What kind of world is this?... A father who doesn't want to have anything to do with his children." Lippe returned to his.

To cheer her up Lippe offers to teach Ruchami to drive. He reveals a secret: Giti often drove his car before they married. "She was a race car driver." This coheres with his giving her control over their new fortune. As for Hanina's disappointing father: "All that matters is that Hanina loves you and you're getting married. Everything will be fine, I promise you."

Ruchami has grounds to doubt fathers: "It's not you. It's all of you." That resonates. "It's all of you" — it's all fathers, all men, the patriarchal structure not just of this religious sect but of all such religions, indeed all such societal and political structures. That is the repressive, systemic authority this drama challenges.

The unseen Hanina's father is a telling addition to the range of fathers: Lippe, Nachum, Zvi Arye, Elisheva's two dead husbands, Gottlieb. All these fathers serve to define the central subject, Shulem, and the patriarchy he represents.

Hanina's father embodies absence. He is literally absent, even after promising to appear, as Lippe was while in Argentina. The later Lippe supports Ruchami but as he does not sufficiently defend her against Giti he is still Missing in Action. Gottlieb does Esti no favours by crumbling at her tears. Elisheva's dead husbands are a haunting presence but physically absent so unsupportive.

Nachum is as absent of soul as he was absent from his mother. His domination of his marriage is implied by the total absence of Libbi's mother. We hear of her twice but as we never see her, she is another parental absence. Lacking any presence, substance or effect, she's the antithesis to the driving Giti. In contrast, the absent Dvora has been the driving spirit of this drama since the start of I,1, as we follow her husband's and youngest son's measures to deal with her loss.

As suggested by these literally absent parents, the omnipresent Shulem is figuratively absent. Selfish, he is not there for his children. He denies them what they need, hindering rather than helping. His tragedy is the central theme: the failure of the patriarchy when it prefers authority over compassion, privileging ruler over subjects.

In contrast, Hanina — to address Ruchami's fears that he may someday leave her, as Lippe did — violates the ban against the groom seeing the bride before the wedding: "I care more about the fact you're afraid." He stops her outside her home to assure her: "I won't ever leave you, not our children. Ever." Here compassion trumps The Rules. As with Yosa'le and the dog (II,11), compassionate youth takes the humane, proper liberty that hardened old authority forbids.

Ruchami asks Giti if she ever forgave Lippe for his abandonment "Whole-heatedly." "Whole heartedly? I don't know if there is such a thing." Then Giti awakens in the middle of the night, rises, doffs her snood and drives away. When she catches herself, she starts to cry and phones Lippe: "I need you, Lippe." As he drives her back she finally says, whole-heartedly, "I forgive you. And I love you." When she drove off, in that unthinking impulse she succumbed to the same urge to flee that Lippe did at the outset. Now she understands him, *sans* judgement.

Meanwhile, Nachum calls off Libbi's engagement and blames Akiva for trampling on their agreement: "He said he wouldn't paint again and would become a serious Jew." He wants Shulem to pressure him, even to threaten him. To upset his brother, Shulem supports Akiva: "Take my son as he is or it's your problem." Nachum blames

Shulem: "You couldn't stand seeing me make a serious man out of your son."

The brothers quarrel on the cab ride to the unveiling of their mother's tombstone! They are violating Malka's dream injunction to "take care of that *pupick,* my child" (II,1)—the umbilicus, emblem of the essential human link, mother and child, brother and brother. At the ceremony Nachum resents Shulem's bragging about his gravesite, between wife and mother. Nachum plots a brotherly betrayal of Biblical proportions. As Jacob robbed Esau of his birth-right, Nachum tricks Shulem out of his death-rite. Pretending to be a Parisian who wants the burial plot because of its view (!) Nachum, through the Burial Society, offers $11,000 for the gravesite.

At home, Shulem tells Akiva yet another of his dubious stories — a pre-Dvora romance, with "Yocheved Gesundheit." The invented name confirms the story's invention. Just as they were about to tell her parents she insisted he tuck his sidelocks behind his ears. That put Shulem off: "A girl who gives you conditions doesn't really want you." So Shulem broke off with "Menukha, I mean Yocheved." Jesus teaches by parable, Shulem by lies. He invents family history. The obvious falseness of this story undermines the weightier one that follows.

Akiva considers his new Motherhood painting his best work. Kaufman wordlessly agrees, rushing it onto the exhibition invitation. Suggesting a television interview, he acknowledges the concerns "you people" have with the media. "What do you mean 'you people'?... I'm the only one here." Akiva declares his independence.

On television with real commentator Yaron London,[17] Akiva is introduced as an unusually young, talented and Orthodox artist. He corrects the critic's Christian reading of his painting. "There is nothing Christian about it. Nor Jewish." It expresses a humanity that transcends religion: "Every painting is an attempt to turn the present into a memory. This painting is a memory of a memory."

In citing "memory" as the foundation of his creation Akiva contrasts to the corrupt Aronofsky (II,8). Where the latter exploits grief

---

[17] Talia Carner notes that artistic expression is excluded from the Second Commandment ban against graven imagery. Critic London didn't get around to saying that on the TV show.

to sell a recording, Akiva's objective is neither a sale nor a recording but an emotional work of imagination. Where Aronofsky records the particular Akiva reaches for the universal. Their objectives are also antithetical — profit from one story vs a truth of mankind.

Akiva's abstracted subject matter coheres with his broader religious spirit. The baby is himself but also his own (future) son, *i.e.*, all sons. The woman is but is not his mother. It's the eternal image of Motherhood, which would include Dvora but range beyond her. As the ducks Akiva was drawing were not the ducks in the pond (I,4). Similarly, Itzikel with the goldfish (II,7) was the universal image of vulnerable innocence protecting essential life, however based in Akiva's memory of Levi Itzhak and his own vulnerability.

When Libbi watches the TV show she is touched when Akiva says he'd abandoned painting until a woman "restored my desire to paint. She restored my desire." Hadassah may have been more instrumental in launching his career as an artist. But it took Libbi's ban to make him realize how important art-making is to him. Repression nourishes what's banned. As Jung observed, "What we resist, persists."

But Shulem is outraged: "All of Geul is talking about my son who paints his mother like a whore in the market." He has not seen the work but "I don't have to see it to understand." That is blind faith — or its diabolical parody. Clearly Shulem has forgotten Rabbi Cheshin's wisdom: "Why fill your head with prejudgments?" (I,5).

Akiva shows him the invitation: "How can anyone even think it's Mom?" The painting does not show Dvora. But Shulem is bent upon posthumously paying his wife a respect he denied her alive. In insisting the image is of Dvora Shulem forgets not remembers her. His actions betray her values.

Shulem reduces art to the parameters of his own religion. As Akiva (like Kaufman) reminds him, "It's a painting, Dad, not real life." But to Shulem: "Everything is life and what we do with it." But it's Shulem, not Akiva, who "doesn't get it." Shulem not his son throws a childish tantrum.

Then Shulem tells Akiva yet another implausible story. Dvora's head covering accidentally slipped when they were entertaining guests. This wardrobe malfunction so humiliated her that she cried all night. As he consoled her then, he leaps to her ostensible protection now.

"You will take back that painting of your mother of blessed memory, you hear me?" Akiva refuses.

"Nachum was right," Shulem says bitterly, "When you paint you care about nothing. You sold us, Kiva. You sold me and your dead mother. And for what?" The selling-out charge soon turns against him.

Shulem's certainty amplifies his ignorance about art (and about Dvora). Akiva painted the universal mother and baby, not any one in particular. The Haredi ban sets their women apart from the world's. This exposed hair reunites them. By evading the Haredi covering Akiva presents the universal mother. Akiva sees the universal in the individual, the eternal in the particular. That is what unites the respective missions of religion and art.

Kaufman, defending the painting, counsels Shulem the way Dvora would: "Be proud of your son. He said wonderful things on the television interview." To keep the painting out of any museum Shulem offers Kaufman the burial-site offer of $11,000 to buy it. Having lost his mother's tape recording by not paying enough, here he overpays for a respectable, responsible work — that he would destroy.

Carrying it home, Shulem assures himself: "No big deal. A gravesite is no big deal." Having lied so often to others, here he lies to himself. As he does when he passes off his self-humiliations with "No harm done." For this is a big deal. Dvora had begged him to buy the adjoining gravesite to preserve their eternal union. He'd resisted; she'd insisted. Now he abandons her deathbed wish — in the guise of defending her honour. His "What matters is only what matters" in II,12 is a bitter echo from I,3.

Shulem has long bragged that he would be buried between his wife and his mother. He valued his gravesite above all the world's riches. He wouldn't sell it for a million dollars. Now he sells this most prized possession — to buy his son's painting, not out of Dvora's pride but out of his own arrogant shame. He buys it to destroy it.

Nachum gloats how he has just exposed Shulem's false superiority. "He's all talk. He sold it!" Years of seething jealousy sound behind Nachum's exulting that "He's no better than me." As for his deception? "He deserved it!" Not knowing why Shulem sold the dear site, he assumes it was for the money.

Nachum's glee repels Libbi: "What? He deserved it? Did Kiva deserve it? Did I?... You ruined what we had by your stupid fights....I want to live with Kiva the way he is. He's good for me. I trust him. I want him to paint." The intercutting of the plot lines suggests a parallel between Libbi's revolt against her father and Giti's escape to Lippe.

In his opening exhibition remarks, Kaufman declares Akiva a groundbreaking artist who is paving his own path, idealizing nothing, avoiding exoticism, to "put reality on canvas — and it's alive and vibrant, painful and touching." Like this drama, especially here.

First Akiva, then the late-coming Libbi, leave his exhibition to drift through the museum. He leaves and she enters under the baleful gaze of his little Itzikel. Beside their bodies we see their abstracted reflections multiplied in the glass. Life like art transforms reality — and should give pause for reflection. Each is doubled, tripled, imaging the fragmentation both of their selves and as a couple, that their union will integrate. As Ruchami's marriage coach advised, "In order for a couple to be complete both halves must be complete."

This couple find refuge in the museum's preservation of an old synagogue. In the last shot, though they sit on the bench, not touching, they have finally come together. Here Akiva achieves the wholeness he envisioned in II,7: in an old synagogue (religion), he can follow his dedication (art) while enjoying a loving marriage to Libbi (life).

Shulem's final scene, the series' most complex, to which the entire drama has built, is rich in paradox. Shulem confronts Akiva's respectful "profanation" of Dvora but then profanes it himself. In putatively honouring her he violates her every value.

The woman's face lights up behind the canvas when Shulem approaches it with a flame, apparently intending to burn it. The face seems to come alive, as the Sabbath is welcomed as a radiant Bride. His *havdalah* candle signifies the end of the Sabbath, its distinction from ordinary time. The blasphemy is not in the image but in Shulem's *havdallah* attack upon it.

Fire is an Old Testament form of destruction *cum* purification. Shulem may feel fire will purify his destruction of his wife's *ostensible* image. But the ritual candle recalls his school-speech remark (I,12): His mother's Sabbath candle tears were not as genuine as her emotions for even her TV friends. However deeply driven, Shulem's burning integrity is another rote act, like his mother's candles, ceremonial, compulsive, not profoundly honest.

Instead of burning the image he paints out the woman's exposed hair. That addresses Dvora's shame in his story. Of course, that story itself seems one more of the lies we've caught him in, especially the demonstrable falsehood of his suicidal aunt (of whom Malka never heard) and this episode's fable of "Menukha, I mean Yocheved Gesundheit." In covering the hair Shulem reduces the universal mother to the Haredi mother. He reductively imposes the sectarian upon the human.

Paradoxically, in trying to make the work more Jewish (*i.e.*, more Haredi) he is making it less so. He amplifies the Christian implication that the TV interviewer suggested and that Akiva denied. For Shulem's slashes of bright blue impose the colour that Christian art associates with the Virgin Mary. Shulem's bright blue conflicts with the grey in which Akiva painted the mother's snood and the dark blue of her dress. Shulem's shade of blue shatters the harmony. His intervention shows his insensitivity to shades, in colour as in morality. Preserving his wife's religious purity compromises her even more.

This scene culminates the interdenominational spirit that has shaded the drama, most explicitly in I,9, with Akiva's "baptism," Shulem dangling the Messiah-like baby on his lap and Eran's dream report that The Rabbi loves Jews and Gentiles alike. Embracing all religions does not diminish any one, but reasserts their common mission — to serve and not to abuse humanity.

Earlier details also reflect upon Shulem's action here. In his yeshiva interview Yosa'le affirms the law that a thief can claim ownership of a stolen object if he alters it. Shulem's over-paint is a theft of the work, even though he (over)paid for it. It is no longer Akiva's vision. As Shulem in effect re-signs the work as his, he aligns himself with the corrupt Fuchs. That fake artist, with his servant, true artist Sasha, established the poles available to Akiva's ambition. Here Fuchs confirms the dishonour in Shulem's spoiling of Akiva's work.

Shulem ruins the painting to preserve his delusion that he is protecting his Dvora's memory. However, in attacking their son's integrity, in once again dividing Akiva and Dvora, and in denying Dvora's wish to be buried eternally with her husband, Shulem is further from his beloved wife than ever. His "honouring her" is a total affront. Perhaps that's why he sobs here. His action is so dramatic yet so futile.

Most of his memories of Dvora — our flashbacks — were not of the happy times he claims. They show him failing her: turning off the phone against young Akiva's calls, distorting his vision, ignoring her requests, whether for new chairs or a shared gravesite, or proving ineffectual, as with her last request, for a chocolate. His disregard for her alive can hardly be balanced by — his present abuse.

Nothing can now make up for his never having told Dvora he loved her. Her warm visits now attest to her love and devotion, not to his. Crying over her dresses, salvaging her kitchen, dumping her unworthy successor, no posthumous service can make up for his neglect when she was alive. Shulem only compounds his living offences when he destroys her favourite son's success. The powerful patriarch proves powerless, hollowed by his insensitivity. Far from the "whole" implicit in Sholem, Shulem is irreparably broken.

As his final action so violates Dvora's values the series' last two scenes bring us back to its first. Shulem in effect consigns Dvora to the deep freeze of Akiva's initial dream. He has still not come to terms with his loss.

But Akiva has grown, from mourning his mother to now starting his own family and career. Where he initially loved the older woman, the mother Elisheva, from whom he would have received shelter and guidance, he now assumes life with the younger, closer Libbi, to whom he will provide those. Indeed the woman are nominally related: "Elisheva" meaning "Promised of God" and "Libbi" being a contraction of that name, to "my beloved, my heart." Akiva has grown up. In marrying Libbi he stays close to his family, community, tradition — spurning the break that marrying Elisheva or Hadassah would have entailed. Were Dvora watching this life on that celestial TV (I,12), she would be proud of her son — but failed by her husband.

Everyone but Shulem gets a happy ending here. The self-unaware, dogmatic and repressive patriarch has caused most of his children's suffering — and his own mad solitude at the end. However, despite everything he did to his children and all that he neglected to do for them, they have survived. Here that constitutes triumph. At the plot center Shulem alone is left the failure, the authority found heartless and powerless. He stands as a condemnation of the cold righteousness of the patriarchy.

After all, a Jew with a dog could be the best kind of Jew, one who cares more for the living in need than for traditional restrictions. There probably were some sages who contended just that. For Shulem showing that humanity then was the rare exception not, alas, his rule.

Conclusion
A bissel un a bissel macht a filleh Shtisel. [18]

This 24-hour drama took us deep into complex characters and relationships. As its particular religious sect represents other societal groups, religious or otherwise, we shift between fascination with that community's difference and our own "shock of recognition."

My critical strategy was to examine each episode for the particular theme that distinctively unites its several plot lines. I've tried to respect the integrity of each of the 24 structures, yet with an eye on how they work in the over-arching narrative.

My reading is clearly not exhaustive. Other critics may well choose different points of emphasis, make different connections, infer other implications from phrase, situation or device. Indeed they may well adduce even from my "evidence" quite different readings. That's the magic of connecting with a drama of such extraordinary richness. I hope my reading is sufficiently based on "evidence" from the text that it's my discovery there, not my imposition upon it. I would be delighted to read corrections, rebuttals, extensions to the interpretation that I offer here. Debate among viewers can only enrich the life of the artwork thus explored. *Shtisel* deserves nothing less than such thoughtful and deepening engagement.

On one point I expect to be in agreement with whatever readers find this book. *Lux sit.* Let there be the challenge of a Season Three — but only from the same creators and with the same depth and integrity. Otherwise, let this family — who have served the thematic functions for which they were created — rest in their peace.

---

[18] Yiddish proverb: *A bissel un a bissel macht a filleh shissel.* A little and a little fills the bowl.

Appendix: Is Thinking the New Sin?

A funny thing happened to me when I joined the *Shtisel* chat sites on Facebook. I was expelled for thinking.

I thought I'd joined kindred enthusiasts. But no. I brought the Jewish spirit of exegesis, parsing a text for its meaning and instruction. That's what I've been teaching and publishing for 50 years, in the popular press as well as in the academic.

Alas, I fell before the impenetrable shield of Fannery (in my Yiddish: *fanerei*). Two *Shtisel* websites wanted only un-analytic appreciation — what contributors liked/disliked — not about what meaning any element might have. A few wanted to dig in, even offering informative ideas. Grateful, I've here acknowledged all I could.

The discussion usually treated the characters as if they were real people. They were considered psychologically not thematically. Rather than examine what we are told of them, there was wild speculation about their life outside. What happened to Levi Itzhak? Why didn't we see more of Adi? Hadassah? And Oliver (the Golem)? Most passionately — what happened to Shulem's dog? The writers should have cleared up these mysteries. If they didn't tell us all we want to know, well, that's their failing.

I retreated to the principles of fiction. We accept the story as given. We don't dispute its "facts." We don't presume to rewrite. Nor to imagine anything we want. The viewer focuses on what the writers have provided, no more, no less. No, not all opinions are created equal. The strength of any reading rests on its evidence from the text.

I took care not to be insulting.

However richly imagined, these characters are not people. They embody and perform specific ideas. What they are is not due to how they were raised but how they were written. Where in real life we forgive people, here we are intended to define them sharply, to judge them and to draw conclusions from that — or we fail the artists.

On *Shtisel: Let's Talk About It* the two administrators soon complained. My pieces were too long. And too frequent. Readers didn't want to be lectured to. My comments prevented them from reaching their own conclusions. A few appreciated my ideas but apparently the vast majority were resentful.

Under a *cherem* I was excommunicated for violating the principles of the community. After a brief "muting," when I refused to stop analyzing the fiction the way fiction is traditionally analyzed, I was officially banished.

So I joined *Shtisel Addicts*, reportedly founded as a refuge from the first site's tyranny. Again, my readers' feedback was usually appreciative. But not by the administrator: "Sometimes I have no idea what you're talking about." Then "How many times a day do you say 'patriarch'?" "I've stopped using it in my marriage," I replied, "But it comes up when I'm discussing *Shtisel.*" For the central figure is a patriarch whose abuse of his authority makes the drama about abuse in repressive systems, especially the patriarchal.

But to some Shulem is the standard-issue loving father and devoted husband. Ignoring the mass of contrary evidence reduces a complex and instructive failure to the cliche Father Knows Best. As I cited my evidence, the admin pounced: "I know where you're going with this. Stop it." Later: "What did Shulem ever do to you? Get off him." Finally: "You have an agenda." Of course, I replied: It's to celebrate with thought a brilliant drama on TV, to try to understand as well as to enjoy it. She expelled me too.

Both sites were Jewish-run with predominantly Jewish followers. As the yeshiva scenes recall, close reading and debate over literary texts is an honourable Jewish tradition. So what has happened?

My banishment for being analytic is worrying. Are we not supposed to think about what we're shown or told? If not in literature, then how will we survive in politics, where the stakes are higher? Will our protective bubbles only admit confirmation of our prejudices? Of misinformation? Is an unsupported opinion as good as a supported one? That's not democracy but its death knell.

As in art the part can carry the import of the whole, in social constructions the macro can paralyze or poison the micro. Apparently America's larger political division has spread even down to website discussions of an Israeli TV drama. That is tragic.

About the author

Maurice Yacowar is Professor Emeritus (English and Film Studies) at The University of Calgary. In his 44-year academic career he was Dean of Humanities at Brock University (St. Catharines, Ontario), Dean of Academic Affairs at Emily Carr Institute of Art and Design (Vancouver, BC), and Dean of Fine Arts at The University of Calgary (Alberta), where he retired in 2006.

His publications include the following books: *Roy and Me: This is not a Memoir* (Athabasca University Press, 2010); *Mondays with Moishe* (humour: lulu.com, 2009); *The Great Bratby* (Middlesex University Press, 2008); *The Sopranos Season Seven* (lulu.com, 2007); *The Sopranos on the Couch: Analyzing TV's Greatest Series* (Continuum, 2002; expanded editions, 2003, 2005; 2006); *The Bold Testament* (humour: Bayeux Arts, 1999); *The Films of Paul Morrissey* (Cambridge University Press, 1993; Spanish edition, 1999); *Studies in International Cinema* (B.C. Open University telecourse, 1992); *Method in Madness* (St. Martin's Press, 1981; expanded edition by W.H.Allen as *The Comic Art of Mel Brooks*, 1982; expanded edition, Crescent Moon, 2015); *Loser Take All: The Comic Art of Woody Allen* (Frederick Ungar, 1979; expanded edition, Continuum Press, 1991); *I Found It At The Movies* (Revisionist Press, 1978); *Tennessee Williams and Film* (Frederick Ungar, 1977); *Hitchcock's British Films* (Shoestring Press, 1977; revised edition, Wayne State University Press, 2010); *No Use Shutting the Door* (Fiddlehead Poetry Books, 1971).

Dr. Yacowar provided the commentary on the Criterion laser disc editions of *Blood for Dracula*, Paul Morrissey (1996; DVD 1998); *Flesh for Frankenstein*, Paul Morrissey (1996; DVD 1998); and *Invasion of the Body Snatchers,* Don Siegel (1987).

For decades he reviewed films in journals, newspapers and Canadian radio and TV. He provides "instant analysis" of select current films on his blog at www.yacowar.blogspot.com.

Dr. Yacowar lives in Victoria, B.C., Canada, with his wife, Anne Petrie (who's not chopped liver herself).

www.ingramcontent.com/pod-product-compliance
Lightning Source LLC
Chambersburg PA
CBHW030858180526
45163CB00004B/1625